TWELVE STEPS UNLOCKED

By

Dell Miller, CADCII &

Linda Miller, B.A.

www.12StepsUnlocked.com

Heron Publications
P.O. Box 1579
McMinnville, Oregon 97128

ISBN: 0615525024
ISBN-13: 9780615525020

Library of Congress registration number TX7-368-654

Acknowledgment

This book is dedicated to all those who have entered through the doors of recovery to achieve the freedom from addiction using the Twelve Steps. Even those who were working the Twelve Step program and relapsed, received dignity and self-respect that no one could take away from them for the time they remained free from addictions.

I once was going to a Twelve Step meeting and an older woman walked in the door before the meeting had started. She asked if anyone knew her daughter Elizabeth, who had been attending the meeting for almost a year. She reported that her daughter had moved to New York and shortly after she relapsed, and had just died of an overdose a few days earlier. She said that when her daughter was living with her and attending the Twelve Step meetings, her daughter reported that the past year was the best year of her life. She said, "I wanted to thank you for giving my daughter happiness back into her life before she passed." There wasn't a dry eye in the house, many of the members embraced her and gave her comfort.

Dell and Linda Miller have been working together at various treatment agencies in the field of addictions since 1988. This book was written in first person perspective from Dell M. with assistance from Linda Miller, providing a balance of experience in this resource for both men and women working a Twelve Step program. The stories that are shared in this book are from people in recovery with whom they have had personal involvement.

Alcoholics Anonymous World Services Inc.

These are the original Twelve Steps as published by Alcoholics Anonymous

1. We admitted we were powerless over alcohol—that our lives had become unmanageable.
2. Came to believe that a Power greater than ourselves could restore us to sanity.
3. Made a decision to turn our will and our lives over to the care of God *as we understood Him*.
4. Made a searching and fearless moral inventory of ourselves.
5. Admitted to God, to ourselves, and to another human being the exact nature of our wrongs.
6. Were entirely ready to have God remove all these defects of character.
7. Humbly asked Him to remove our shortcomings.
8. Made a list of all persons we had harmed, and became willing to make amends to them all.
9. Made direct amends to such people wherever possible, except when to do so would injure them or others.
10. Continued to take personal inventory and when we were wrong promptly admitted it.
11. Sought through prayer and meditation to improve our conscious contact with God *as we understood Him*, praying only for knowledge of His will for us and the power to carry that out.
12. Having had a spiritual awakening as the result of these steps, we tried to carry this message to alcoholics, and to practice these principles in all our affairs.

From Big Book of Alcoholics Anonymous, How It Works, pages 59, 60.

© A.A. World Services, Inc. Reprinted with the permission of A.A. World Services, Inc.

In some cases, where other Twelve Step groups have adapted the AA Steps as guiding principles, they have been altered to emphasize principles important to those particular fellowships, to remove gender-biased or specific religious language.

Most of the alternate wordings are in Step One and Step Twelve in various other Twelve Step programs. Such as Step One: We admitted we were powerless over _____- that our lives had become unmanageable.

Table of Contents

Introduction

This book has been written to give a fundamental, nuts and bolts understanding of how the Twelve Steps work for men and women in recovery. There is clarity in presenting an understanding of not only addictions, but how Twelve Step programs aid in restoring recovering addicts' lives. It was written by a recovering alcoholic and addict, who also has been a Counselor in the field of addictions over the past thirty five years.

We will look at how addictions grow into taking control of our lives and a simple understanding of how denial replaces self-awareness. This book examines characteristics of addictions that seem to follow certain patterns, which will be reviewed in depth. We will show how addictions deteriorate the fabric of our relationships and ourselves. We will give a clear understanding of the architecture of the Twelve Steps with insight into motive and purpose of how the Steps can be implemented. The stories of those who have had the courage to make the program part of their lives are used for illustrating how the program works. This book breaks down the Steps, offering tools in building a higher awareness of our actions to improve the quality of our relationships with others. Another precedent shows how the program aids in being in charge of our health and physical recovery.

The flavor of what recovery is about is accented throughout this book. You will see the program from the inside out and how the networking of the fellowship is an integral part of working the Steps. We have also contributed to a website for downloading Step worksheets to aid the reader in their recovery at www.12StepsUnlocked.com. This book will give an in-depth understanding of how the culture of recovery works outside of the Twelve Step meetings. It offers an understanding of the resources which are a "must know" to experience what recovery/sobriety can be. The material is insightful, and sometimes offers the true joy and humor that accompany recovery. This book introduces a refreshing perspective which may offer answers to some of the hardest questions we approach in working our sobriety/recovery in the Twelve Steps.

Understanding the Core to Addictions

In this chapter we will begin by giving the basis for the book in layman's terms, on how addictions operate and progress to control our actions. We will also review how Twelve Step programs assist in bringing stabilization to this chronic illness. We will provide insight into the realm of addictions and recovery. This will offer a blue print for any individual seeking recovery from alcoholism and addictions.

The fundamental principles behind addictions are that we use the substance or behavior from which we are addicted to change how we feel. Instead, we need to be using relationships with other people to change how we feel. Twelve Step programs in its' simplest form helps people to build relationships with others to change how they feel. The Steps are worked in conjunction with others to assist the individual in regaining healthy relationships with others. Yes, the Twelve Steps have spiritual principles, but they are gained through the relationships with others. The purpose isn't to build a spiritual program through the Twelve Steps, but it is a bi-product of working the Twelve Steps through our relationships with others.

We will show how the fabric of relationships weaves through our lives to build meaningful, personal values to our experience. We will give you a basic understanding of how communication with others is a vital part of a fulfilling life.

Our social values are the same as our personal values. We believe that we inherently have the same rights as others. We start out our lives with a blank slate, expecting that the rules we have for others are the same as we have for ourselves. This is how our minds perceive the world around us. This process sets the stage for developing unconditional relationships with other people which opens the door for intimacy to grow. Healthy relationships are built on unconditional expectations with others because it assists us in generating positive self-esteem and regard for others. For example, the effort we take to build an honest relationship with a Significant Other gives us the bi-product of positive feelings about ourselves and our relationship.

Humility is the concept of self-value that renders us equal to others and is the building block for our spiritual connection with others. So the term 'the door opens both ways' is the basic building block for relationships. An unconditional relationship could be known as a relationship that exists when the standards and expectations are mutually agreed upon in a respectful manner of equality. The effort to build these relationships through honesty and communication strengthens the fabric of trust and intimacy between one another. This information flows freely in unconditional relationships with others. Underlying this is a fundamental spiritual connection with other people.

A conditional relationship is created when we use control or being controlled as the primary justification for being in the relationship. Our behavior in constructing these relationships with others is known as character defects. When we create addictions we're no longer being filled with the sustenance from our relationships with other people, we are using substances to artificially mark the significance of a moment. As we are doing this, we splinter off our human relationships and that leads to building character defects.

So now we're not looking at just the initial problem of the addiction – the drinking, the drug use, the addictive behavior – we're delving into the subsequent problems that spill over into our personal relationships. In counseling people over the past thirty five years I have found the most serious devastation of addictions is the isolation that the person feels and experiences in their relationships with others. This creates an emptiness and vacancy of a spiritual connection with others. That emptiness then triggers us to try to create a relationship with others through control or being controlled, which is the basis for our character defects.

This innate connection with others is lost when we begin to abuse substances or get into compulsive behaviors. We lose the ability to have unconditional relationships and replace them with conditional relationships. As the person begins to abuse substances, relying on them to change how they feel rather than their personal relationships with others, they lose the intimacy and trust they had. These conditional relationships give us a perceived sense of purpose and meaning for being in the relationship or not. For example, through control of another person I determine the right to be in a relationship because they need me or through giving up my control to another person, I need them. To avoid personal and emotional contact with others, I may find excuses to be left alone.

When we think of what the gratification is that the person receives from addiction, it can be different for different people. Some see the benefit being a feeling of being invincible; another may be to numb them of conflict, stress and pain; to another a way to release the build-up of emotions. This perceived sense of reward fuels the continued obsession with addiction. As we indulge in the use of the substance or behavior to give us this reward, we have expended resources that we normally would have used in our relationships for the benefit of getting high. I no longer have to actively work on myself to feel good; I can synthetically build that with alcohol/drugs or addictive behaviors.

Denial and its Origins

When my drive to use a substance triggers a loss of control in my behavior and causes harm to someone, instead of admitting to it I then justify my actions. This is because to set things right would take away the possibility of the reward being available. These justifications for our actions allow us to continue to perceive ourselves in the same manner, suggesting we are living with the same values of others. Since we are still living by these set of expectations for ourselves and others, we can proceed with our abusive behavior without feeling guilty. We have our cake and eat it, too. This false perception of self builds in our lives to develop into Denial. Remember, De-nial is not just a river in Egypt. Denial occurs in everyone, you could say that everyone lives in glass houses.

I was having dinner with my sponsor and his wife, both are psychologists, and as I entered they were having a conversation that everyone lives by two sets of standards. I listened to their conversation and stated that I thought I was pretty self-aware and I take great effort to be aware of my behavior in my relationships with others. I asked for an example how it pertained to my life and my sponsor asked how I felt about people digging up Native American burial sites and taking the loot for their own benefit. I said that I thought it was grave digging and frowned upon people taking items that were sacred to a culture's heritage. He then said 'you hike around a lot and you have shown me arrow heads and pottery chards that you have found, what makes you think they weren't part of an unmarked burial site?' I got it.

With all of us there are exceptions we have made where we have justified our personal actions. In being able to see a different perspective, we often have to ask for an objective view from someone else. As part of alcoholism or other addictions, people usually slip into patterns of denial which we automatically do to justify our actions.

Our conscious awareness of ourselves is determined by our value. *I once went to hear a presentation by Dick Van Dyke, who at that time in the mid 1970's was noted as recovering from alcoholism. He was asked what the most valuable lesson was in his recovery. He responded by saying that his values changed based on his changing needs.* An example of this may be of a woman who is partying with friends, drinking and using drugs. When she becomes pregnant she may change her values or expectations of herself and stop using during her pregnancy. *Thirty years later in an interview with Robin Williams, who had just went through treatment for his alcoholism, he was asked why he went into treatment. He said he 'couldn't lower his standards fast enough to keep up with his actions.'*

The reference I am making here is that in life we are born with a consciousness and we govern our behavior by what rules we expect others and ourselves to act by, known as values. In our perception our rules are the same for ourselves as they are for others. Our ability to follow those expectations gives us a perceived clarity of who we are pertaining to our present life experiences, as in our reflection in the mirror. As time goes on in our life we make certain exceptions to ourselves because of the desire or satisfaction that we prefer to continue to experience. Because we are social beings it is a priority that we have the same expectations of others as we have for ourselves. So in order to continue with the behavior we have to justify our actions in some way. Through gradual exceptions we make to our behavior, we develop an equal amount of excuses and justifications to compensate for them. As time goes on, eventually the image we see in a mirror is different than that of what other people see.

I had a man in treatment named Jack who came into group saying he was extremely angry at his ex-wife and she was setting him up to relapse. Jack reported that he was going to have visitation with his five year old daughter last weekend and his wife refused to have her stay the weekend at his apartment. Jack reported that part of his commitment to stay sober was for his daughter, and his ex's actions are causing havoc with his recovery. A peer then responded to Jack, that he is in the same boat having visitation with his own daughter. The same peer then said, he knew Jack well and that they worked and drank together for years, and he knew that Jack was committed to his recovery and sincere about remaining sober. His friend included that although he is sincere about his recovery he still has buddies come over that bring alcohol to his apartment and Jack hasn't gotten the strength to tell them to get out. The peer then said 'Don't you think your wife has got the same intentions as my wife has, that she just wants your daughter to be safe?' He nodded and exclaimed that it was his problem, not hers that got him in these circumstances. Often these choices are very gradual in our life, and as our actions change we don't even notice the layers of justifications, rationalizations and excuses we have made.

I once had a rancher in treatment. During group an assistant of mine, who started facilitating the group, asked the rancher how much he drank a day. He responded "two drinks of scotch" and the assistant replied in a comment of disbelief saying, "Two drinks are all?" The rancher firmly said "Yes, that's how much I drink a day". The assistant was going to move on and I intervened, asking the rancher 'How big are those drinks, are they whiskey shot size?' He responded, "No, I have those tumbler size glasses I keep in the kitchen". I asked how big they were, and he responded about so big, gesturing about 16 oz. I asked if he used any mix, and he said "No, I like the taste of scotch." I asked if he used ice and he said "No, I like my scotch room temperature." I said, "So, you drink 32 ounces of scotch a day?" He replied, "Yes, two drinks." He wasn't trying to hide his use, but the methods of concealment were in having to ask the right questions to get an accurate answer. This would be considered a guarded reaction to the question. These layers keep other people out so that we can continue the self-gratification of our addictions. These defenses also act as a prison, which doesn't allow the addict to escape from their addictions.

The defenses we develop as part of addiction and life experience become ingrained into our personality. It becomes a threat to strip someone of these defenses because they are losing a sense of their identity. The Twelve Step program assists people to let go of their past character defects as they surface in their lives and replace them with other, more functional assets.

The streets of Minneapolis were my proving ground for my addiction/alcoholism during my younger years. I went through a residential drug rehab program in 1973. The treatment center did a comprehensive psychological profile test on me called MMPI. I thought that when I sat down with the psychologist as she read the results that it appeared she was frightened of me. She reported I had a sociopath/psychopath personality. I asked her what that meant and she said I would most likely be in institutions the rest of my life. I stayed sober after living in a halfway house, attended Twelve Step meetings and went back to school. In college three years later, I was in a clinical psychology class and they reported that the MMPI test was revamped to adapt to mostly young men who grew up around a lot of violence. Those men who had anger and apathy as a defense mechanism were miss-scored as sociopath/psychopath personality types. I took another MMPI when I was sober twelve years and the test results only showed obsessive compulsive tendencies, which is characteristic of recovering alcoholics and addicts. The apparent psychopath/sociopath personality was not there. If a person is a true sociopath, those tendencies would continue throughout their entire life.

What I am saying is that defenses can be so ingrained into our personality that it may take a gradual process to replace. On a humorous note, the psychologist was right, I have been working in treatment centers, so in institutions pretty much my entire life.

An example of perfect denial, I was working as a resident intern at a State Hospital, a patient who was schizophrenic believed he was Jesus Christ and walked around with a sheet wrapped around him. There was another Schizophrenic who believed he also was Jesus Christ that had arrived at the State Hospital. I wondered what the encounter would be like if they ever met. One of the residents ran into the ward stating that the two men who believed they were Jesus Christ were in a verbal fight in the courtyard in the middle of the grounds of the institution. I ran out and so was half of the State Hospital observing these two individuals reaction, they both were screaming at one another claiming that the other was an imposter.

Patterns of Addiction

There tends to be a common theme in the patterns of alcoholism and addiction that individuals construct in their relationships with others, which coincides with their pattern of abuse. Although not everyone's pattern of addiction fits within these parameters, these patterns seem to follow characteristics found in post-traumatic stress, which are fight, freeze or flee. Often you may find some addicts having more than one pattern of abuse. These patterns were referenced in my previous book: Re*Union - Healing Our Victim and Offender Patterns, copyright 1993. The fighter would be identified as the controller/offender pattern in relationships in which they receive an uplifting feeling of invincibility, a feeling of "be all you can be", in their addictions. Freeze would pertain to the addict in the victim role in relationships in which they receive the feeling of numbing their emotional, physical pain through their addictions. The flee reaction would be identified as an isolating/binging pattern in which the addict benefits from a release of emotions through their addictions. All three patterns identify the general parameters of addiction, which people with disabilities, mental health issues, chronic pain, trauma, cultural factors or other dynamics can contribute. We refer to alcoholic as addict or alcoholism as addiction often through the book to simplify the message.

The Fighter Pattern

1) The Fighter - This controlling/offender pattern develops by setting unrealistic expectations on their partner, maintaining control in the relationship and guaranteeing their place in it. It is difficult for the addict to look at their behavior as an offender, because it denotes being a criminal. The term offender in this fashion is used to identify controlling, self-serving behaviors which cause damage to others. The controlling behavior becomes more exaggerated as their addictions build in their life.

The offender, having no expectations for their own behavior, sets up a self-serving pattern of abuse of substances to feed their own gratification. They will often use "the high" for their personal gratification. This reward supplements the lack of intimacy in their relationships with others. In the progression of their controlling traits, the person in this role will continue to seek power and authority over the people they are closest to.

The addict places rigid expectations on ones they are closest to, which gives them the opportunity to dump their anger on their partners. Anger is used by them as the primary release of pent-up emotions. The individual uses anger for release of all their feelings in a purging fashion. They release fear, anger, loneliness, and sadness in one outburst. The addict in this manner is able to transfer their negative emotions to someone else, usually the people they are closest to. By expressing emotion in this way, they do not allow themselves to become vulnerable. The addict justifies their behavior in ways that blocks them from seeing their own actions. In fact they don't see their behavior as abusive. The individual does not see their behavior as offensive to others, but as self-care and self-protection. In most circumstances the person in their role would stop their behavior if they saw their actions as hurting people they love. This has been the case for years, the most common form of addictions are control/offender oriented. Abusers tend to surround themselves with others who accept their control, which reinforces their justifications for their behavior. These individuals use their charisma, intelligence and power to position themselves as the leader/authority figure.

Another controlling pattern is caretaking others, believing that they are doing things in the best interest of others. They are not taking into consideration the receiver's views on the matter. They are excellent managers and workers because their capability in this area serves as a position of power. They realize the world doesn't revolve around them, but they believe because of their abilities they deserve special entitlement recognition and reward.

In their reliance on the addiction to fill their lives, they have lost ability to have unconditional relationships with others. Again they use this position of control in relationships to justify their right to be in a relationship. Without these relationships they feel un-needed and that they are an outsider. These individuals are certainly not going to exhibit their control issues in every relationship, but in those that are most significant.

People in Twelve Step recovery have been successful in bringing balance back into their lives. When people drink, their inhibitions lower and they become more aggressive. More often than not I have heard people report that when they are drinking, they can be aggressive and abusive to people around them and the ones who suffer the most are their family.

A client of mine reported that he thought he would never strike a woman, but due to his drinking he found this circumstance happening in his relationship with his wife. After one incident she called the police and he was subsequently ordered to participate in anger management and treatment for his alcoholism. This was how he came to be in treatment with me. He acknowledged awareness that the unrelenting amount of hours he put into his two jobs placed pressure on him and he began putting unrealistic expectations on his wife. In his closing assignment in treatment he reported him and his wife and children have been closer than they had been for years. He reported his attitude was negative and impatient toward the time his wife and family expected of him when he was in his addiction. His worst fear was falling back into the same attitude he had before his recovery. We talked about his involvement with Twelve Step meetings being an insurance policy to continue to reinforce those same values he was introduced to.

Yes, people in recovery can see the difference and view addiction almost as a horror story of them being Jekyll and Hyde. *An elderly man who had come into treatment appeared kind and loving in his interactions and could not see how his behavior had caused harm to his wife. After all, he was just having a few well deserved drinks to offset his life in retirement. He was asked to talk to his wife about what her perception was. She brought out a tape recording that she had made of him when he was drunk the previous summer. He was appalled at his sharpness and ridicule of his wife when he was under the influence of alcohol.*

In some cases simply stopping the pattern of addiction can curb a lot of their behaviors, but some character defects are more deeply embedded. Of course no one would give up such a powerful position in a relationship without some type of intervention consequence that leads them to recovery. This could occur due to family, job, legal, or medical consequences. In Twelve Step recovery we call this hitting bottom. The addict has to literally be cornered in order to face their problem. Once their addictions have been confronted through some type of intervention they may be ready to enter recovery. This is a moment of clarity that is very special to the recovering addict. They are in one of the most fragile positions they have been in their lives. Their hardened defenses begin to dwindle away as you look into their softened eyes seeing pain and emptiness. They change from hardened, tough individuals to teddy bears. It is essential that they have access to resources to assist them in their road to recovery. If resources are not available they could slip back into the darkness of their addictions. They may enter through treatment or counseling and become introduced to Twelve Step programs.

It is essential for the addict to have family involvement in their recovery. I have found that there is a substantially higher level of recovery with family involvement. The addict has to look at the unrealistic expectations they had for those closest to them. They also need to look at how their addiction lacked rules that were needed to govern their behavior. This awareness allows them to put their expectations of others and themselves in a realistic proportion. These individuals tend to be open in disclosure about their issues, which makes it easier for the person to move from a state of compliance to acceptance of having a problem. Still, denial is a factor that contributes to their inability to see their actions.

For example: A client reported that the way he ended up in treatment was due to him being drunk and getting in an argument with his wife. He ended up, in his anger, taking his gun and shot the sofa. When asked where his wife was, he then admitted that she was also sitting on the sofa at the time.

Twelve Step programs and counseling can aid the individual in healing those damaged relationships. We need to clean up the wreckage in our own back yards to build a strong recovery program.

The Victim Pattern

2) Freeze Pattern - The first category we will define is a victim in a long term adult relationship with an offender. Victims must acknowledge the controller/offender's authority in the relationship, which guarantees their place in it. We may not think of this as control, but by staying in the relationship with the offender they are exhibiting a choice, although the benefits don't seem appealing.

The victim gives control over to the offender which offers them the convenience of not having to make any major decisions. The control they're exhibiting is guaranteeing them a place in a conditional relationship. Their interactions set them up as being the fall guy in the relationship. The victim sets rigid expectations for themselves and no expectations on how the offender treats them; or they are afraid to hold them accountable out of fear of further abuse. In some cases acknowledging it is their fault in the relationship, prevents any further retaliation from the offender. The lack of consistency between the rules and expectations for themselves and others creates a window of vulnerability. The rigid rules and expectations for themselves encourage a self-fulfilling prophecy of chaos and helplessness. They will use their addiction to numb the emotional pain in their lives.

The victim is in a balancing act a lot of the time in their relationship. They tend to be the carrier of the burdens for their partner they are vested in. I am not saying it is a conscious effort for the victim to continue in the relationship, but through their innate lack of self-esteem they tend to believe this is the only type of relationship they deserve, can get or simply that there are no other choices available to them. The victim uses their drug of choice or behavior as an addictive crutch which will either manifest itself into further isolation or into another abusive relationship. This does paint a disturbing picture of how the person becomes imprisoned in these relationships.

Certainly there is hope for the addict/alcoholic who gets into these patterns. They can develop meaningful, nurturing relationships with others in recovery. Many women's Twelve Step meetings focus on self-empowerment and codependency awareness. Of course women aren't the only addicts to suffer from victim patterns in relationships and solutions are found for all who are searching for recovery. This book gives a balanced perspective and understanding of victim dynamics and how to break free from those character defects by working the Twelve Steps.

Brenda was a chronic alcoholic and was married to a Doctor who was prestigious in the community where they lived. He was verbally and physically abusive toward her. Her drinking was the usual excuse he used to abuse her. One day he came home and she had been drinking. She reported that he beat her until she went unconscious in a coma. He left her lying on the floor in the kitchen. A colleague of his dropped by the house and found her 36 hours later, lying on the floor in dried blood but still alive. Her husband was not convicted of physical abuse because he denied he had beat her, stating she had been intoxicated and someone else must have done it. She entered treatment and he filed for a divorce. He had ample proof of her alcoholism through her history of DUII's and other factors, so he was about to win the case of not providing any support to her. She came back into the office for a visit a year later, she was sober and happy and going on a cruise with another woman in recovery. She reported her ex-husband had died from a stroke just before the divorce was finalized and she got everything.

Next is an example that reflects a man in a victim role. *A client named John was in treatment for his substance dependency and his significant other (S.O.) was known to be verbally and physically abusive towards him. He reported that his S.O. came home intoxicated and began to break things in the household that were his. He realized that the conflict was that he was getting sober and his partner was not. He took a bed at a local Oxford House, which is a recovery half way house, for sanctuary to continue his recovery. In treatment he was able to recognize that he was the scapegoat for his partner's ridicule of him, which put his partner in a position of control in the relationship. After a year sober he recognized that his attempt at reconciliation in the relationship was impossible and moved on with his life.*

Victim and Offender
Common Characteristics

Both victim and offender relationships develop a conditional relationship with one another. They develop into two sides of the same coin, as one cannot exist without the other. When people establish victim or offender identities in their lives they also establish strong justifications for having them. Both roles are rigid and people believe they cannot change their identity: the victim, with the sense of hopelessness; and the offender, with the denial of pain.

Offenders conceal their wounds, never allowing them to be exposed to heal. The victims have no boundaries to their wounds, allowing other sources of conflict to irritate them, never allowing them to heal. The inflexibility in rules and expectations that both victim and offender present shows alienation in their relationship with others.

Clearly the rules and expectations they have for themselves are not equal to the rules and expectations they have for others. The impact of this alienation from others impairs the ability to develop any true sense of intimacy in relationships. The loss of spiritual connection with others voids the potential for compatibility and balance in our relationships. In order to co-exist in our relationships we create a sense of direction through these victim and offender patterns. In our behavior as an offender and as a victim we will create an interaction which we control.

As a victim, we use internal control of our environment by assuming responsibility for the outcome, thus creating a sense of position and negative empowerment with others. Offender behavior utilizes external control to repel others, while victim behavior uses internal control to attract others. Control is a major influence in the victim's fight to survive, fed by their need for approval from others. Victim and offender traits are also progressive and will continue to consume larger portions of our true self. These masks block our ability to gain nurturing relationships through trust and intimacy. The unending peril of unmet needs and unresolved trauma perpetuate further development of the behaviors.

The victim identity in contact with an offender identity will establish a dependent/authority relationship. Here the victim identity recognizes the offender as a source of power or authority, while the offender identity will recognize the victim as a dependent. It is a dance which clarifies the identity of each other. They are truly in a hostage relationship with one another. We justify being an offender and/or victim, saying that is the price we have to pay to sustain a valuable relationship. The person builds a conditional relationship through sustaining unrealistic expectations of each other. One of the founding fathers of a mediation model was Paul Forgash, PhD. I was working with him at a program called Victim/Witness in 1984, which was a pilot program for victims of crime, and is now in every County Attorney's office in the country. I was using his method of mediation to counsel alcoholic/addicted families and was very successful. Paul Forgash was a mentor of mine and I asked him personally how he came up with the concept. He told me they were basic concepts of mediation he had found while working at the Los Angeles Police Department on a pamphlet for hostage negotiation.

Relationships that develop in the alcoholic/addicted family systems create hostage relationships with their partners and family members through victim and offender patterns. The offender has rigid expectations of others around them, and the victim has rigid and high expectations of themselves.

Victim of Circumstances Pattern

The second category is the victim of circumstances. This is a pattern a person may encounter, that creates a change in our lives of which we are not in control. This could be due to physical disability, mental illness, trauma, chronic pain, or losses. Yes, losses happen to all of us, but when we use addictions to help cope with those losses, we close off any ability to gain support from others to share our grief. We become stuck in the grief cycle and the only ones who give us comfort are ourselves and our addiction. We can find no resolution because we are contained within the walls of the isolation of addiction. The person uses to numb their pain, which is only a temporary solution. In fact those who use substances often find their grief is intensified by their use of the substance.

Often when addicts go through a loss, their substance abuse intensifies in time, duration and amount consumed. The person gets stuck in self-pity, which could be termed self-grieving. In order for a person to get through a loss, they need others to share their grief.

When we bury a person we have pall bearers to assist in carrying the deceased. When we are in our addictions we have one pall bearer, that is us; and we have no ability to move on through the stages of grief to get to acceptance. The victims of circumstances who are addicted will be stuck in a victim pattern because they have no way of getting resolution to move on in their lives. There is resolution for these individuals through working the Twelve Step program.

The person coming to terms with their loss sees the opportunity for new life to begin. Their transformation in recovery offers them new meaning for their losses, which strengthens their commitment for recovery.

A man named Jim had Polio at an early age, leaving half of his body affected. He had one arm that had very little muscle mass. He was brought up on a farm and left school at around fourth grade to help out on the farm, which left him illiterate also. Because of these conditions in his life he had an inferiority complex, but used his humor as a way of charming others. His life experience placed him in a victim pattern and he used alcohol to numb the emotional pain in his life, placing him in a downward spiral into alcoholism.

He went through a residential treatment center in Minnesota and got sober attending AA. He worked at a treatment center for adolescents for twenty years. He was sober about twenty five years when his Polio developed a second crippling factor in his life through Post-Polio Syndrome. This syndrome is common for aging polio victims causing a decrease in capabilities, and for Jim caused a spiraling effect into depression.

I talked to him several months after that and he and his wife had purchased forty acres of land. They cleared five acres in the middle and were in the process of building a new house. His energy and mood changed 180 degrees and his health issues had stabilized. I asked him what triggered his change. He said when he got sober it was a turning point for his new life in recovery. He said when this new problem came up he thought, 'Well, it looks like time to start all over again'. Jim said he used the Twelve Steps to deal with his medical condition which he was powerless over. His health stabilized with his attitude change once he began the process of charging forward with this new direction in his life. In the past 7 years since then, his Post-Polio Syndrome has stabilized and remained in remission; and he continues to live his program of recovery.

Another pattern of being a victim of circumstance is growing up in a household with an alcoholic/addict, and /or offender/victim. Children brought up in these family systems are caught in the grasp of the chaos of a dysfunctional family, which they had no choice in.

Often there was no intervention for these children to escape and they developed skillful defenses which allowed them to survive.

When these children discovered alcohol and drugs, it gave them the only outlet that took them away from their pain. In adulthood, adding a substance or addictive behavior creates almost instant satisfaction to their complex lives, creating addictions in another manner. In this process the cart is before the horse. They grew up in the chaos of addiction, leaving them empty and using alcohol and drugs were the only thing missing in their lives. The term "Rehabilitated" acts as a factor in adjusting a person back to a normal set of values in which they had lost in their addictions. But if a person grew up in a family with addictions, they may never have known the possibility for unconditional relationships. These individuals sometimes wonder what is normal anyway. For these people, the person coming into recovery has to experience the changes in their life, sacrificing what they knew at least to survive in relationships for something they didn't know. We call this term "Habilitation" because they are adjusting to a lifestyle and a different set of values that they never knew. The principles of the Twelve Step programs are still the same for these individuals to apply in their lives, but this doesn't mean it's any less reachable for them. Their reach for recovery is no further away than anyone else.

I myself grew up in a household where these factors were present. I was told by professionals that my chances for recovery were possibly unreachable. I simply chose not to believe in their statistics and that I had as much opportunity as anybody else, and I succeeded in my recovery.

People who have been victims from any set of circumstances can be left with Post-Traumatic Stress and need to seek professional help to aid them in their recovery. Twelve Step programs aid the individual in coming to terms with their losses and trauma by implementing the tools that are written in this book.

Chronic Pain Pattern

Chronic Pain is a contributing issue for a lot of people with addictions, which is part of being a victim of circumstances. People with chronic pain are not at fault for their condition, but physical and emotional pain can be overwhelming. I have worked with many individuals who had to accept that their pain was a part of life which they would have to manage indefinitely. As a Counselor, I have found that working with their Medical Doctor and/or Naturopathic Doctor is a necessity for recovery to take route. Using the Twelve Step model program, I have seen countless individuals who have chronic pain take control of their lives again.

People with chronic pain often initially have circles of support other than the substance- they have family, friends, career, spirituality, hobbies and other interests. As time goes on the person withdraws from these circles of support because the intensity of the pain is preoccupying their thoughts. The person begins to lack the ability to benefit from these relationships. In the back of their mind they may be keeping track of how long it had been since their last dosage of the pills, because the pain is never gone. This turns into an obsession around trying to find a solution to their pain. They may turn from one doctor or procedure to the next looking for the cure, which they never find.

Their search turns to a temporary chemical solution. I have participated in chat rooms for chronic pain, and often I have heard people asking what drugs are working for them. Yes, it is perfectly natural to try to find a solution, but what this pattern of thinking brings about is the mental addiction to substance. This only brings about a temporary solution. This obsession to find a fix for the problem begins to cut away the important relationships in their life leaving them feeling alone and isolated. This is addiction. The solution that I have found for most of the clients that I have worked with was to find daily hope and to find a way of constructing their lives that they can honestly live with. With the nature of pain, it is random and can emerge in intensity after a period of calm. There are no cures or quick fixes, it is a lifestyle to which the person has to find what fits with their needs on a daily basis. People with chronic pain who are addicts often will find it necessary to continue to take pain killers for managing their pain. The person in recovery has to redefine the value of relationships in their life and rebuild their lives with the love and involvement with others in recovery.

While I was working in Tucson, AZ, a man called me, about his sister who had chronic pain and was addicted to narcotics. He asked me to set up counseling with her as they were re-locating her to Tucson for her health, and he was leaving later in the week. I told him the earliest I could get her in was next week, but that I would be at a Twelve Step meeting tomorrow night. I told him if she came I could meet her and get her connected with others in recovery. He said she was blind, so I told him he could bring her to the meeting; then he included she was in a wheel chair. I thought he was possibly making excuses for her to not come to the meeting. I told him that I thought it was wheel chair accessible, but if not we could assist her in getting into the meeting. I went to the meeting that night and after the meeting the man's sister said "Yeah I just want to know who the @#% is who told my brother to carry me into the meeting." I immediately took a liking to her. She had chronic arthritis and diabetes, but got into recovery. I called her the bionic woman because she had every joint replaced in her body including all her knuckles. She faced insurmountable odds in her life including getting her sight back only to lose it again, yet remained in recovery. She went back to school and became a pain therapist assisting other people to cope and live to the best of their ability.

I had another client who had chronic arthritis whose hands were disfigured by the disease. At an inpatient facility where I worked, another therapist thought he was intolerable because of his anger. I understood that with the amount of pain he lived with, who wouldn't be angry. Anger is simply energy that can be tapped into for helping people making change in their lives. He had an amazing family that became an important part of his recovery. His family participated in a segment that I contributed to on the "Sobriety Game" in an article on 'Alcoholism and the Family,' cover story for Newsweek in 1987. By applying the principles of the program, he came out of his shell of alcoholism and addiction, transforming himself into a loving, caring man with enthusiasm toward his recovery.

Isolator/Binging Pattern

3) Flee pattern - A scenario in the flee effect of relationships is the individual who isolates in their relationships with others, separating themselves from any intimacy. These people are identified as isolators/bingers. A binger in this context prefers to drink or use alone, using in a compulsive manner. Their control is exhibited through isolation, by doing so they no longer have to live by the expectations of others, only their own. The individual relies on the substance for their emotional needs. They develop a relationship with the substance almost as if it were their significant other. They continue to maintain relationships with others to function in society, but rely on the substance for intimacy. These individuals may become effective managers in their business relationships with others or with their family or friends. These individuals have high expectations about their performance and may or may not be aware of having a problem with substances or behaviors of addiction. They rely on their substance or behavior to fulfill and release their emotional needs, which trigger them to conceal it in some manner. They may try to control their environment to maintain control of their emotions. This of course is an impossible thing to accomplish so stress begins to build in their lives. The individual uses internal control of their emotions to suppress the feelings. The person will use the substances to release their built-up emotions. They present a facade that their lives are okay. In fact, they may exhibit an external profile of an easy going personality.

This outside image is a camouflage to cover up what is going on inside of them. They have done so well that they cannot even see it. This individual builds a sense of secrecy about themselves in their intentions to others, to protect their relationship with the substance.

They tend to be organized and maintain relationships with other people, yet they fall short of sharing their true feelings with others. I haven't been able to find clear data on how often this happens. This is a more rare form of character defect and addictive patterning that occurs. This individual will drink, use substances or addictive behavior with others, but will prefer to use alone. Often they will leave early from a party to drink or use in the privacy of their own homes. These individuals who close the curtains and drink or use in silence are bingers. They build up emotions in their personal life because of their rigid expectations of themselves, others, or events out of their control. It is a pattern that was set up for self-protection, triggered by victimization or through self-entitlement in protecting one's source of gratification. This can also be seen when there is unavailability of the partner in meeting their significant other's needs. For example a spouse stays at home with their children while their partner works out of town for long periods of time. The significant other may gradually develop a relationship with the substance to meet their needs.

When they drink they release their emotions and feel comforted. Some isolators/bingers have reported that once they ended their binge, the next day they felt a tremendous amount of guilt and remorse. These deep emotions can be translated into physical signs of distress. No matter what the outcome of the circumstances, the binger starts the cycle all over again.

The isolator/binger often relies on their cognitive abilities to manage their emotions and develop successful careers. They may try to hide their drinking or abuse from others by masking the smell, or hiding bottles. We often see these individuals as functional alcoholics or addicts, but the outcome is still the same as they become further isolated from others.

Usually from some type of outside intervention the person is confronted on their addiction. The initial intervention/confrontation usually triggers intense shame about their actions, because they have been excellent illusionists about the issue in their lives. Due to their high expectations of themselves they usually are a lot harder on themselves, often moralizing about their actions. This moralizing behavior is not an asset, but rather keeps them in denial of an honest portrayal of their addiction. Yes, because of the moralizing they will often respond out of compliance. Now that it is out in the open they tend to put an effort into making changes, but have a difficult time adjusting to acceptance of the problem in a realistic way.

The adjustment to attending meetings with others and sharing about their issues can meet with resistance. These individuals some-times have difficulty adjusting to Twelve Step meetings because they can't relate to the out of control stories that people share at these meetings about their lives.

Bingers, in fact, are too much in control of their lives and rely on their addictions for any release of emotions. I have seen these patterns of usage vary depending on the individual. Patterns may vary from people who drink on a daily basis to ones who drink periodically. They may go into binging activity or a cycle of abuse and then abstain for one week to nine months. The length of time that the person uses also varies from days to weeks. The person has developed a cycle of use that needs to be intervened on. Their cycle will trigger another binging pattern to begin. This cycle of abuse becomes a natural process for them and needs to be interrupted for recovery to begin.

Often redirecting the individual towards getting involved in service work can be a motivating factor because they again become strong contributors. Referring the binger to a professional Twelve Step meeting can assist them in building relationships with others, because they build relationships with others as associates. Involvement with a counselor in recovery may help them in developing stress management skills in learning to express their new found emotions.

Professional Twelve Step meetings are set up for professionals in the community that are concerned about their confidentiality. You will find higher functioning alcoholics and addicts attending these meetings.

I had a client who had previously been sober for eight years, and came in to address her relapse. Her drinking patterns were hidden, drinking alone at home. Gail had several different high profile careers which all ended due to the direct results of her drinking. She was intelligent and appeared motivated for making change. She had developed a physical dependency on alcohol and was provided with detox treatment. Several times she relapsed in the process of her stabilization from alcohol. Her family was involved in the intervention and provided support to her recovery. Her drinking patterns were creating further isolation in her life, hiding bottles, masking the smell and making excuses to miss family and social activities due to her intoxication. She stabilized and at present has four years in recovery, and is in college pursuing a degree in counseling.

Another individual was a Longshoreman who reported not drinking for six months to one year. Whenever he drank, which lasted several days of intoxication, he would usually get a DUII. He had nine DUII's by the time I began working with him. I saw him recently and he reported having about ten years sober since his treatment and has remained sober successfully since. I told him that I use his case history in my education series to explain binge alcoholism and it has helped countless people. He left, grinning ear to ear.

Sometimes you find people who enter Twelve Step programs and get into a cycle of periodic relapse. In some cases this has translated into another cycle of relapse which changes their regular pattern of abuse of substances into a binge addiction. They may get one month to a year sober and then relapse periodically. They stay consistent on the length of time sober before they use again. These individuals get caught up in a cycle of not being able to correct their behaviors that trigger this course of action. Their sincerity for recovery is there and their motivation in working on their issues is significant.

The impasse that these individuals get themselves into may need intervention from other areas, such as mental health, nutritional, exercise assessment, stress management or spiritual guidance in order to correct this.

I had a client who could stay sober up to a year at a time before relapsing. He had a pattern of binge addiction, and was an excellent manager of a ranch with up to twenty workers. He went to a Naturopath Doctor and found he was allergic to wheat along with several other food items. After changing his diet and developing an exercise program he found his coping capability with stress was much more manageable. It assisted him in remaining sober, along with his involvement with Twelve Step programs.

There are people who are dual diagnosis with other types of mental health issues which need to be addressed by a mental health practitioner in conjunction with their Twelve Step program. I have seen others simply treated with an anti-depressant, which helped curb stressors that would trigger relapses. Others have successfully changed this relapse pattern by their involvement with churches or other spiritually supported groups.

Playgrounds and Playmates

To break free from our addictions we must change our playgrounds and playmates. To change well routed addictive behaviors in our life we must cut out the outside resources that reinforce our behavior. We are social beings, and as such our values are influenced by the group of people we associate with. A male may show respect to women in his relationships, but when he goes to work at a construction site in a downtown city, he most likely will be hooting and hollering at the girls walking by with the rest of the construction crew.

Most people who are alcoholic or addicted will be triggered by outside circumstances. If they move to another location, they will build the same type of peer group to reinforce their addictive behavior, as they have integrated the process within themselves now. Some substance addicted people or alcoholics isolate themselves in their usage. Their patterns in social relationships don't apply so much because their relationship is with the substance primarily to change how they feel.

Most people who don't abuse substances would use alcohol or mood altering substances to enhance their relationship with others. A bottle of wine between two friends in the evening might be an example. In this manner the alcohol could lower their inhibitions to talk about the more personal details of their lives. As time goes on we may begin to use the substance as a crutch, shifting our emphasis to use our friends to enhance our relationship, with the substance. A client once said that she used alcohol as a crutch until she became a cripple. This crutch is created when we expect the chemical to create the intimacy rather than our relationship with the friend.

Our friends often become using friends. In my peer group of using friends, some may have used less than me, and some may have used more than me. Through association of that peer group, we all felt immune to the consequences of our drinking or using behavior. The exhilaration that we experience in the use of the substance with our peer group gives most of us a false sense of intimacy with that group of people. But, if we quit using with that group of people we tend to lose the association of the intimacy because we aren't using with them.

In spending time with those peers when they're using, we begin to experience the Big D, that's not Denial - it's feeling Deprived. Because we are not with a using group of friends, we tend to feel isolated within the group. Breaking ties for a while is usually recommended to give a person a sound foundation in a new lifestyle.

This break in our relationship feels a lot like betrayal to our old friends. I went back to associate with my old friends the first time I went into treatment, and encouraged several people to attend Twelve Step meetings with me. Their enrooted lifestyle sucked me back into using with them within a few weeks of being around them. That group of friends was greater than I was as an individual, I had to admit.

The group of using friends I had was like family to me. I agreed to cut those friends loose as part of what you would call a relapse recovery plan for the first year of my sobriety. Yes, we will probably test those relationships, but the best thing to do is get some time in recovery first. Then you can get together at a restaurant for a meal or someplace where it would be unlikely for friends to be using. I believe the longer we are abstinent/sober we get more aware and a lot smarter.

I remember a close friend who I hadn't seen in a year contacted me while I was in a halfway house. When I was drinking with him I thought he was smarter than any of us. When I got together with him sober, I got the feeling that he was dumber than a box of rocks. Well, where did that put me when I was using and thought he was smarter than any of us?

I had a client who reported he had moved away and got sober. After two years he moved back home and got together with an old using friend, picking him up to go out for coffee. His friend was sarcastic, ridiculing him, so he asked why he was treating him that way. His friend said 'that is how I always treated you.' He said he then remembered and took the old friend back to his house, and has never seen him again.

In developing better awareness in recovery, we are sometimes able to evaluate later that some of our relationships in our addictions were destructive to us. Often, we perceive people as friends who in the relationship weren't offering anything to do with our best interest, other than our sharing of the substance we were using. Personal choices in relationships give us the reward of stimulating our thoughts and actions. I developed a variety of relationships from mentors to friends when I first entered the Twelve Step program. I get smarter by hanging around smarter people.

The toughest time a person usually has is the first year of recovery, because they are giving up an old peer group and building new relationships to replace those lost. They are going down a new path in life, one that they are not accustomed to. This is a time that the recovering person is most vulnerable and needing support. It is often a tough time for the recovering person because vulnerability is a trait least appreciated. I usually describe this as *"defiantly dependent."* The person knows they need other people, but this feeling often surrounds the emotional state of vulnerability which is threatening and uncomfortable. Their senses tell them to run away rather than taking the risk to get closer to others. We often see this as being a weakness while others see it as a as strength in us to face the truth about ourselves.

I was giving a lecture at a Veteran's Administration alcohol and drug rehabilitation program and a man came up to me after the lecture. He said he remembered me from a Twelve Step meeting two years prior that we both attended, and he named the location. I remembered him and that he went for at least five months. He reported it was strange run-

ning into me again because he had since relapsed and went to prison. He reported something I had said in a meeting stuck in his head, and that inspired him to go into treatment. I thought to myself, 'what pearls of wisdom did I lay on this guy?' I asked him what I said and he stated, 'it wasn't what you said, you had just broken up out of a relationship and you were totally messed up for weeks, but you were still clean and sober.' He knew I was a die-hard alcoholic/addict.

That wasn't too pleasing for me to remember because I was a mess and needed help from others. In general, it is that which other people see as strength, when we only see ourselves being a burden to others.

Our relationships with peers at work can be a trigger for most of us. Simply conversing with co-workers can be a trigger when they start telling using stories. These can be known as war stories because they are glorifying the experience of their patterns of abuse. Our part in the conversation builds our own glorification of our use, which can trigger a craving to use. We all get into war stories about our use, even old timers in the program start to tell about their exploits when drinking or using, at Twelve Step meetings. The important thing is to catch yourself glorifying your prior use, and then slip in what consequences occurred during the situation. You will find those who were in the conversation moving away and you distancing yourself from the glorification.

I had a client that was sober for eight years and worked as a lumberjack. He reported all of his peers on the job at lunch break would glorify themselves about their use; he then would inject his own war stories about drinking. Because he was joining in with stories about glorifying exploits of use, he was leaving the door open to relapse. He was invited over and over to join them at the bar. He eventually went out with them, they left the bar and he stayed almost until closing and got a DUII.

Closing the door rather than leaving it open is part of our recovery. I use the terminology of a six inch addict sitting on your shoulder who is the alcoholic/addict; if we leave him/her have room to grow they will take every bit they can get.

We tend to migrate towards friends who will justify our behavior. In some cases, the friends we grew up with stay as our life long loyal friends; because we never grew up, neither did they. It is difficult to see "using friends" as not being real friends. Often I have seen clients who are in a time-warp with their peer group with whom they went to high school or college. They reinforce each other with their patterns of abuse of alcohol or other substances. They could be in their mid- 30's, 40's, or 50's age group, etc.

One group of men I worked with were friends since college. Their drinking endeavors lead them to buying a bar together and they drank up the profits. They continued their friendship as drinking buddies for over twenty years. Over several years I worked with this group of men, and all three eventually got sober. They built an elegant and popular restaurant on the river front and from their prior obsession, the bar they built as part of the restaurant was probably the most beautiful bar I had ever seen. Yes, sometimes using friends can get sober and be part of our support system for recovery.

Impact on the Family

In the relationship with family we need to address the obvious effects the impact of our drinking and using has on them. The people who tend to suffer the most in addictions are within the relationships with family. As a counselor, I have seen it beneficial for the person in recovery to have involvement with family in their treatment. I use the term transference as a reference to the pain absorbed by family members.

An example I use is: I have a friend, who is very funny man, and I invited him out to dinner with a minister, priest and chaplain. During the dinner the friend proceeded to tell a dirty joke that was in poor taste. I felt embarrassment for his behavior, because through my association with my friend and his shameless behavior, I then experienced the shame for him. This transference was not resolved until I confronted him later in the car; probably giving him an understanding how his behavior had impacted our relationship.

Then the transference would pass to the appropriate person, this is called confrontation. Transference in addictions occurs when the addict/alcoholic, through avoidance, does not assume responsibility for their actions. When this occurs, those closest to them, "the family", pick up the tab. They take responsibility to cover up for the addict/ alcoholic's actions or lack of actions. The price family pay to stay involved is absorbing the chaos of the addict they love.

There is balance that exists in the roles and responsibilities shared in a family. When a family member becomes addicted they abandon their responsibilities in the family, which throws the balance off among the others. Some may react by getting angry, others may enable the addict. This additional obligation placed on the other family members puts the priorities in their life on hold, to take care of the addict. If the addicted member gets better down the line, they will then assume responsibility for their role in the family and the family adjusts back to their natural patterns.

To begin to understand the addicted family system, let's first look at the selection process of their partner. When a person has a pattern of loss of control in their patterns of substance abuse or addictive behavior, the partner they select will confront their actions or reject them due to them not changing.

Sometimes in the selection process of a partner we find someone who also has a substance abuse problem. What better way than to have a partner to share your love for your substance of choice. Of course there is the issue of who I can blame into taking over my lack of responsibility. This will usually generate in whoever may be able to maintain a dominant position in the relationship. If physical force is the factor, often the man will maintain the dominance in the relationship. Other factors may contribute to the selection process, but one usually comes out on top. The passive role is essential in transferring responsibility for the other to carry both of their emotional luggage. If both parties are pretty even on their ability to hold their ground, the responsibility may flip flop from one to the other. Another scenario may be when the addict/alcoholic finds a partner who through some defect of character themselves, has the inability to confront others. They feel they have found their true love. Their partner's condition could have been triggered by abandonment issues or other factors in their own life. The alcoholic/addict will act out and the spouse will begin to confront the partner with their feelings, stopping just prior to holding their partner accountable for their actions. When the spouse lacks the ability to confront, they rely on manipulation, guilt or blaming others. The partner may try to manipulate the circumstances to get the results they want, but it never happens. For example, she sees him spending time with his friends so she goes out to buy some camping gear so they may have time to themselves. He invites his friends and gets drunk next to the fire with them and comes back to the tent and passes out. The addict avoids dealing with any of their negative emotions, which then transfers to their spouse. The significant other becomes an emotional packhorse for the unresolved feelings in the relationship.

Another behavior that is familiar for the family members is *passive aggressive behavior*. This may happen when the partner begins to confront the addict. Due to the addicted partner's drinking, using, or addictive behavior, their significant other's anger has been building up. Their anger comes out in a sideways manner, instead of a direct confrontation. Once they see disapproval in the eyes of their partner they withhold their anger and revert into a victim stance with no boundaries. This sets the stage for retaliation from the addict, in which they feel justified in their attack. Trying to communicate without the skills to hold the addict accountable is like throwing gasoline on the fire.

There is an escalation in the conflict in the relationship between the alcoholic/addict and significant other as the progression of the disease of addiction occurs. The verbal, mental and possible physical abuse which is part of addictive relationships continues to build. Sarcasm is Latin for 'cutting of flesh', and the ritual of bickering back and forth in a relationship gives a sense that there is some substance to the relationship rather than emptiness that is left by the addiction. As the argument increases, the personal ridicule increases in verbal and mental abuse. The consequences of verbal, mental and physical abuse are among the wreckage left in addicted family systems.

When I was working with victims of domestic violence, there was a group of women I was working with who had been seen at least once in the ER for physical abuse. I remember it being fall of 1984 because the day before one of our groups, the movie "The Burning Bed" was aired on TV which was about the victim getting payback on their perpetrator. I was a young counselor and somewhat naïve, I remembered that night because the women were pumped up as a result of watching the movie and you didn't want to be the only male in the group. I asked the question: what was worst, the physical abuse or the verbal abuse? They all said unanimously that the verbal, mental abuse was the more destructive. I asked why and their reply was that 'when you've been beaten so badly you require hospitalization and the perpetrator will stop for a while. The verbal and mental abuse, however, never stops. You are told that you don't even have a right to have a thought in your own head. You become a worthless slave'. I will never forget those words. Violence is a factor that is real in family lives.

Often I have heard alcoholics/addicts early in recovery exclaim that they never hurt their family, only themselves when they were using. Even when we were just depressed and they were trying to get us out of the depression, families suffered because we weren't attempting to make change and the responsibility fell on them. Remember by not taking responsibility for ourselves in our addictions, the responsibility falls directly on the shoulders of those closest to us.

The energy of the abuser becomes focused on those who are active participants in their addiction, their using friends. Often the partner may say, if you put half the energy you put into your relationship with your friends with me, I would be happy. They simply see that they are in a relationship with someone's back walking away from them. In their frustration they reject their partner and say they have had enough. When this happens, the transference of negative energy switches back to the addict, they feel remorse and regret thinking they have lost the one they love. The behavior of the addict at this point is a familiar one. It reminds me of the movie "Blues Brothers" when Belushi is cornered by his old girl friend who has finally caught him and is ready to kill him. He takes those famous sunglasses off, bats those pearly blue eyes at her, and holding her in his arms he says 'you know you love me' and she responds 'yes', so he immediately drops her on the ground and walks away. The addict uses the same charisma that won their partner over in the beginning. Once they got you hooked promising to make changes, they turn around and continue the same actions. The spouse of the addict has become codependent to their partner with spiraling consequences.

It is at this time that the significant other usually develops into what I call a "secondary addiction". The partner, locked into their apparent unrelenting relationship, develops into a way of numbing their own feelings that they are carrying. It may be 'forget it, I'll just drink and use with them', or 'I will use anything other than what they are using, so I'll get a prescription for Xanax from the doctor', or by using food, sex, gambling, addictive behaviors, etc. One client reported that after seeing their partner's binging pattern resurface she would give herself permission to go to the casino and spend whatever was in their account. Even after the addict gets sober in a family there is wreckage that needs to be resolved. If the family member of an addict doesn't get the help they need, sweeping it under the carpet doesn't resolve anything.

I once took over a group for a Medical Doctor who was going back to school to become a Psychiatrist, and was moving out of the area I had just moved into. It was a couples group for people who had been sober for more than five years. While sitting in with the Doctor before he left, he introduced the group to me. There was a cute couple who were in their 70s. The husband had been sober for six years, but when he was given positive feedback from a peer in the group, his wife cut him down. I took over the group and she did the same thing again. I asked her if there was a reason for it and her response was "I was wondering when someone was going to say something. I've been coming to this group for nine months." I asked her to elaborate on her answer. She reported they had been married over fifty years and I thought 'isn't that cute' inside. She continued that he was a hard alcoholic and then she leaned forward, physically shaking and said 'he was a mean alcoholic, too'. She said 'you know when the children were young he would beat me right in front of the kids. When he got sober no one asked how I felt about it.' I then asked the words, "So, how do you feel about it?" You could have cut the energy in the room with a knife, she looked at him and said in a calm voice "I guess I'm here to make him pay", as he nodded his head.

When the addict gets clean and sober a lot of families and addicts try to sweep it under the carpet. Letting out the grief of the past gives an opportunity for renewed commitment to the relationship to begin.

A daily program is about recommitment, so using that same process of recommitment to our present relationships helps us to build a relationship in the present. Sometimes you can have all the information in the world and have quit the addictions and the relationship may not get any better. A relationship requires nurturing if it is to grow.

The Twelve Step meetings and its' fellowship offers a conduit for making personal life changes. The interaction that renders this possible is, first, the ability to share about our personal experience and second, receiving input or feedback from others in recovery. Although it is highly recommended not to give advice or crosstalk at a Twelve Step meeting, giving personal feedback to peers in recovery occurs as part of the fellowship outside of meetings. Through these relationships we share a nucleus of being part of a group where we are sharing about a primary issue, being our addictions and recovery. We change our playgrounds and playmates to find recovery. We transition from relationships with other users who shared the same values as we had, which kept us stuck. We build relationships with other people in recovery which reinforces the changes in our values.

Johari Window and Twelve Step Programs

"Johari Window" by Joseph Luft and Harry Ingham can give us insight into how communication skills in self-help groups work. I have used this illustration in demonstrating how Twelve Step meetings enrich our lives. A window divided into four squares is used for this exercise as seen in diagram A.

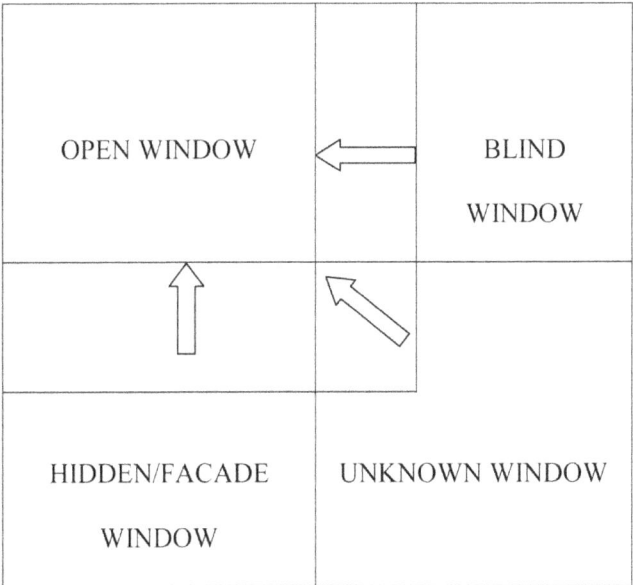

OPEN WINDOW ←	BLIND WINDOW
↑ ↖	
HIDDEN/FACADE WINDOW	UNKNOWN WINDOW

Diagram A

The upper left hand window is the open window of communication. This is the free flow of information between us and members of the fellowship. We discuss this free flow in context of unconditional relationships. It also deals with our conscious state of awareness. By sharing information openly with a group of people, we bring it to the forefront of our minds where it becomes part of our here and now element. The size of this window is based on open flow of information. People who are in addictions usually have a smaller open window of communication because that space is being occupied by elements from the other three windows. So, when we share this information with others we develop self-awareness and see new possibilities in our personal lives. This information is then accessible in making choices about changing our lifestyle.

Next is the blind window of information. This window is in the upper right hand corner. The window of communication is one that others can look through and see our behavior, which we cannot see. This is often described as denial or subtleties of our actions that we are unaware of.

For example, I remember being in the office with other counselors at a treatment center and I was having a bad day. One person said, "You sound angry today," and my immediate response was "I'm not angry, I'm just frustrated." Then I realized that I had fallen into the same trap that I have seen others in as I was confronting them on their anger or justification.

A two-way mirror is another way to look at this. We see our reflection as normal, but when we receive feedback from others, they have a different view. The person giving me feedback may not have an accurate picture of my actions, but it is a view from outside of our perspective. I always say, "If one person says I've got a tail, I may not believe it. But if two or more say I do, I'd better turn around and see if it's wagging."

Often, because of social etiquette, people will not share negative reflections about our behavior. To prove we really want to hear what people have to say about us, we have to demonstrate a teachable attitude. If we are aloof or defensive, people are not going to tell us the truth. We need to ask questions like: "What do you see about my actions that are stopping me from getting through the impasse I am having." Fair-weather friends tell us what we want to hear, but people in recovery will tell us what we need to see. It is important to find a peer group of people who are willing to share with us that which will help us in our recovery, mentors who share the same goals of recovery that we do. I generally have four or five people in my life that fit this bill. I've often said that it takes a hand full of people to change and shape a life in recovery. I know if I call them they will stop and take time to help me on my specific issues.

These people are willing to jeopardize our friendship in order to be honest with me if they see that I am slipping into relapse or probable difficulties in my life. Where do we find these people? Usually at Twelve Step meetings, other resource groups, churches or out in the community, but mostly they are people who are in recovery themselves. When people give me feedback about my behavior and I am able to accept what is apparently true in my life, then my open window of communication becomes larger and the blind window gets smaller. Being open to feedback is essential. It may fit or it may not, but I won't know unless I look at it. I use the term "try on the feedback and if it fits it fits, and if it doesn't it doesn't."

The third window, the hidden facade window of communication, is in the lower left hand corner. This is information that I know about myself, but no one else knows. There are specific reasons why I would withhold information from others.

1) I risk being accountable for my actions.
2) I fear if you knew certain things about me, you would reject me.

Fear of abandonment and the desire to please others are reasons people do not want to share about themselves (their experience or their true feelings with others). When attending a new Twelve Step meeting it is common for a person to have fear or insecurity in adjusting to a new situation or relationship. As the person feels more comfortable with the new group of people or person, they will disclose more information. Peers in recovery will support the person to break through the defenses that are blocking their ability to share with others. This puts a person in a position of having to jump into the interaction with the group and share about himself or herself. This new information about the person then becomes part of the open window of communication. This is a good reason to go to a meeting until you feel comfortable with the people in it. Don't just go once and then drop out.

The fourth window, in the lower right hand corner, is known as the subconscious or unknown potential of the recovering person. This is information that neither the group nor the person is aware of. This may be in the form of early childhood memories that have been blocked by layers of defenses or unknown potential creativity or inspiration that has remained docile or undiscovered. It could also be a flame or passion for discovery that was transferred to our addictions. Once we begin to develop unconditional relationships, then our confidence and personal power in our life experience builds.

We get the balance of interaction with others because we are teachable by receiving feedback and working on personal disclosures. In sharing our experience, strength and hope with others we become part of the resources that the group has to offer. When I was struggling alone with my addictions, I could not see any other options. As part of a group in recovery, I have an abundance of strength and resources available to me. This resource is like changing from 110 electrical powers to 220. That light which was dim, the unconscious state of awareness, now illuminates the other elements that I can use as resources in my life. The unknown potential is now accessible in small quantities as we broaden our involvement with others.

I had a client who came into treatment for his alcoholism because his family had requested an intervention for him. I asked him what I often ask clients: "Was there something prior to his alcohol abuse that he had stopped doing?" The exercise is to get them in touch with any passions they may have blocked in their life. He said when he was in college he studied Art and he was told he had great potential as a painter. However, when he got into the business world after college, he quit. I asked him why. His response was that he made enough money to drink in the eve-nings and on weekends and he lost his desire to paint. I asked him to pick up a canvas and some acrylics, oils or watercolors. He brought in a paint-ing the next week, and asked with a big smile, "Well, what do you think?" It was a picture of a whiskey glass half full of milk. I'm not an art critic, so I just said "It looks good to me." He said he couldn't stop painting after he got that first piece done and it was giving him a sensation of vitality. It was opening up an untapped resource. He got sober after that and won a national archives award for the best entry in his category and has won various other awards over the years.

It is common for people not to be aware of their potential. As they experience success, they move into achievements that they had not imagined possible. The section of the unknown window then becomes part of the open window of communication.

The person often begins by being a newcomer or teachable in the group. This is a normal part of the process of learning about the resources that are available to them. They open the window of communication to take in information, but may not disclose much about themselves to others. This impedes the process of the per-son becoming a vital part of that group. A person does not make a commitment to being a part of a group until they invest themselves through self-disclosure. The person may sit in the back of the room and when it comes time to share they pass or keep their information impersonal. The group becomes imbalanced if the person doesn't eventually adjust to becoming a contributor to the group. If this continues after a person has grown accustom to the group members as a participant, peers from the group will in a cordial way pressure the person to share more. If the person doesn't begin to share, they never become part of the group and they will drift away.

In another set of circumstances the person becomes comfortable disclosing their personal feelings and thoughts to others, but is hesi-tant to listen to input from others. This could be construed as the offender pattern, or the "bull in the china shop" behavior. This cer-tainly interferes with the group process. The group as a whole will have to confront the person on their behavior, which usually results in the person either adjusting to listening to others, or leaving the group.

Another contributor to offender behavior, which I call the "wolf in sheep's clothing" is the person in a care-giving role with others. They become the caregiver of others in the group, or mother hen of the group. This person is focused on everyone else's problems, often giving good advice, but fails to take assistance from others in the group. This person often will share for a lengthy period of time, much longer than others. This can cause the group to become imbalanced. Often the group will come up with their own solutions to these problems, which will usually bring these members back into a working balance in the group. In a Twelve Step meeting it is important to have elder members of the program offer their insight, but no one is any more important than the newcomer in the program.

I have heard on rare occasions an individual demand that the newcomer not share in a meeting for the first few months, and to shut up and listen. My response to that in the past has been "If that were true AA would never have started because in the beginning, Bill W. and Dr. Bob, the founders of AA, would have never gotten sober." Again, if you are uncomfortable with specific Twelve Step meetings with certain members having a strong personality at a meeting you attend, you can easily resolve this by attending a different meeting.

Now there is the large open window of communication and opportunities are recognizable on a "here and now" basis. With the resources that are now at our fingertips, we are able to make decisions that are more in line with our personal potential. We sometimes call this "process networking" with others. When we look at the differences in the windows of the practicing addict to the person in Twelve Step recovery, the person in recovery has a large open window of communication. They have a multitude of options available to them. The addict has a small open window of communication, not seeing any solutions to their problems. Often I have heard people who are active in their addictions state 'there is nothing else to do in this town but drink or use'. There are other possibilities, but they are closed off in their awareness of any alternatives.

Sponsorship, the Essentials of Being Teachable

Going to Twelve Step meetings is one facet of the program of recovery and the glue that helps us to combine that experience in a personal way is getting a sponsor. A sponsor is a mentor in the Twelve Step program who helps you work on recovery. Sponsorship is the bloodline of recovery and it can be traced back to Bill W. and Dr. Bob., the founders of AA. The selection of a sponsor is an important step in our recovery which is not to be taken lightly. Basic rules are that the choice needs to be:

1) A person of the same gender. This narrows the gap in finding someone that has went through similar problems as our own in family, friends and society.
2) A person with long term sobriety, being stable at least a few years in their recovery.
3) Choosing someone who has had a sponsor, and is working with their own sponsor is an important part of finding the right one. You want someone who is invested in their own recovery, not just yours.
4) A person that appeals to you who has taken effort in making changes in their own life successfully, that you can relate to.

There are pamphlets on sponsorship through various Twelve Step meetings available at the meetings, such as Alcoholics Anonymous, Narcotics Anonymous, etc.

It is difficult and humbling to ask someone to be your sponsor, as you want to find someone who not only talks well, but walks it also. I have suggested many individuals ask someone who has been around meetings for a long time, who they would recommend for a sponsor. These people are usually known as "old timers", and would know who to suggest for a sponsor. This way you have someone else's knowledge of the individual with whom you are going to invest your trust.

In the relationship with a sponsor, we are able to share the more intimate details of our personal experiences. It is important to build a relationship with another person who has resources which will assist you in your recovery. Usually a sponsor will go through the Steps with you and help you build up a recovery support system outside of meetings.

The sponsor, as a whole, will be there to help work on the Steps and to spend time outside of the meetings on a weekly basis. Even getting together for coffee, the two of you can discuss the urges and triggers you may be experiencing. It's a good idea to get together at least once a week and have additional phone contact throughout the week. It's necessary to have their phone number for your ability to call when having a crisis; or just to follow their recommendations of Step work to use as part of your program. There is no money exchanged. They are there for you in the same way their sponsor was there for them.

When I first came into Twelve Step recovery, I got a sponsor who was an old timer in recovery. I initially worked through the Steps with him. I also, simultaneously, had a sponsor who had been sober for several years in recovery, but was closer to my age and pattern of substance abuse. He helped me make adjustments in changing my lifestyle, letting go of my old friends and developing healthier outlets. Both sponsors helped me in different issues. Five years later I changed sponsors when I moved to Arizona and again later in a move to Oregon. Even in stable recovery it assists a person to have a sponsor to continue working on ourselves in remaining teachable.

A sponsor may recommend that you go to 'ninety meetings in ninety days.' This tradition of attending daily meetings for the first ninety days is helpful in building relationships with others in recovery. Using Twelve Step workbooks with a sponsor also is helpful. Your sponsor will recommend methods of working the Steps; the key here is to be willing to follow direction.

We imprint moments in our life by reviewing an experience we have had in an interaction with someone else, by looking at what actions they had in the relationship and what our actions were in the relationship. This can be understood as measuring our personal value system.

A young doctor who went through counseling with me came to visit me on his two year sobriety birthday. He stated that self-esteem has been building in his life as a result of reflecting on the actions that he took and seeing that he was living within his value system. He stated 'by looking at my footprints which I have made in my life in recovery, I can see that I am living the life I wish for myself, which gives me satisfaction and self-esteem.'

Recovery is found through the courage to face our life on life's terms. Change is inevitable in life and to embrace the opportunities that change brings is what Twelve Step recovery has to offer.

A mentor of mine, Irene W., used to say that her recovery was like holding onto a tail of a comet. So now if I am fear based, my projection of the outcome would be that I could either be vaporized by the sun or smash into a moon by holding onto the tail. In the light of possibilities, while holding onto a tail of a comet everything that goes by me is something that I haven't seen before.

Step One

We admitted we were powerless over substances or behavior – that our lives had become unmanageable.

The First Step is our beginning foundation of putting the puzzle of our lives back together again. Step One is the only Step that most Twelve Step programs have changed or altered in wording, enable to focus on the addiction that they primarily cover. We begin by breaking down the two characteristics identified in the First Step, being powerlessness and unmanageability.

We will examine what addictions filled in our lives to create powerlessness. This understanding will help to break misconceptions that we may have had that addictions are a moral deficiency. By getting clear information on how addictions build in our lives, we can then better understand how to halt them.

One factor that complicates our ability to move on from addictions is the temporary gratification or release we get, which is normally not present in our lives. When we think of what the gratification is that the person receives from addiction, it can be different for different people. Some see the benefit being a uplifting feeling of invincibility, 'be all you can be"; another may be to numb them of conflict, stress and pain; to another a way to release the build-up of emotions. This perceived sense of reward fuels the continued obsession with addiction.

It sounds simple, but this process of getting our emotional, social and spiritual needs met from our addiction is usually a gradual process for most of us. As we indulge in the use of the substance or behavior to give us this reward, we have expended resources that we normally would have used in our relationships, for the benefit of getting high. I no longer have to actively work on myself to feel good, I can synthetically build that with alcohol/drugs or a compulsive behavior(s). When my drive to use a substance triggers a loss of control in my behavior and I hurt someone, instead of admitting to it I justify my actions. This is because to set things right would take away the possibility of the reward being available.

Usually, in weaving through our life experience, we gain a sense of self confidence, or a sense of reward in accomplishing goals. The bi-product of that "good feeling" is similar to the reward we may get when we get high from our addictions. We begin to expend the time and resources that we used in our personal responsibilities, for the quick fix we get from the use of substances or addictive behavior. The benefit we get from a substance replaces the benefit we receive from sharing our feelings with others. As time goes on, we rely on the substance or behavior to change how we feel. We turn to a substance or behavior to get a similar reward or relief, however temporary.

We then begin to rely on that substance or behavior to change how we feel, because it seems to be a more reliable way than relationships to get that reward. In addictions the substance becomes our main resource for changing any of our emotions; we feel sad, mad or glad. This reliance on the substance to change how we feel rather than our relationships with others takes a toll on our emotional, physical and spiritual condition. The First Step brings into reality the impact this relationship with the addiction has had on our lives. This is usually demonstrated by our impulsive abuse of the substance or behavior.

Most addicts and chemically dependent people have varied patterns of loss of control. Some appear to have a total loss of control in their substance abuse, which is late stage addiction. More common are periodic losses of control that cause negative consequences in people's lives. Admitting we have this loss of control is admitting to powerlessness. These patterns of loss of control need to be identified on how they apply to our own lives. When people look at the First Step, which states 'admits that they are powerless over the substance or behavior,' most will interpret powerlessness as weakness or like a child's sense of being helpless.

An adult's perception of powerlessness, however, could better be defined as a limitation that the person has developed in his or her own life. Adults, even though they have a sense of powerlessness, can recognize what the limitation is and find the resources to work around the problem. Often, however, our pride gets in the way of looking at the issue or issues of the limitations in our lives. We try every conceivable alternative until we are left with the one set of circumstances that will correct the problem. We may switch to another substance or switch from hard alcohol to wine; we may move to another location; we may pick a new set of friends; we try to do everything but stop the use of the substance or compulsive behavior.

This unmanageability can be identified as external and internal consequences which have occurred as a direct result of our loss of control in our substance or behavioral addiction. The first part of unmanageability is external consequences which are self-evident. Now, if we are in a state of avoidance and not willing to admit to powerlessness, then there will be additional external consequences.

This causes unmanageability in our lives. If we took someone who was diabetic and he was not willing to recognize that he had a problem with this disease and he didn't change his diet, what would happen? He would get progressively worse, right? There is personal loss and pain as a result of loss of control. As addictions progress in our lives, the amounts of consequences also grow.

A gentleman reported that the worse consequence he had in his life was being incarcerated for a Driving Under the Influence (DUI) citation and waiting for his wife to come pick him up at the county jail. I thought to myself, "That's his worst consequence? I've spilt more than this guy ever drank." But then he went on to say that when his wife arrived, he could see in her eyes that he had become a stranger to her. When his children greeted him back home, he could tell they were looking at him to see if he was intoxicated or not. He could tell that they were apprehensive and did not know what to expect from his condition. After hearing this man's story and watching his experience in coming into recovery, it gave me new insight. I saw that he wasn't a light-weight, he was a genius in doing something about his problem before it took away the most precious thing he had in his life, his family.

The second part of unmanageability comes not from external consequences, but from internal motivators that kept our addictions thriving. An example is a sense of entitlement, thinking we deserved this in spite of the cost, or that we deserved no better. This exaggerated sense of esteem is often called grandiosity, and the lack of esteem is called worthlessness. These attitudes in our relationships place us at arm's length. The core beliefs that we had while in our addictions fed our character defects. We used these character defects to continue to create a self-fulfilling prophecy, that change is impossible or that change wasn't necessary at all.

It is important for us to understand with clarity that these patterns of thought influence or control our actions. Our character defects are built out of our fear for survival or a continuation of how we were raised. We use what resources we have to establish a sense of functionality for ourselves. These patterns are identified as victim, offender and isolator characteristics. They are part of the mainframe of the work known as character defects, which we will be clearing up through working the Steps.

Being a chronic disease, addictions are also progressive. They may come on fast or gradually, but it is inevitable that they will get worse. We have seen the insanity of addiction in other people's lives, vowing never to allow it to happen to us, but then it did. I have seen many people struggle with their patterns of powerlessness in their lives, from those at the beginning stages of alcoholism to the latest stages.

I was working with a man named Jack at a homeless shelter. He remained abstinent for nine months and then relapsed. For the next seven years he was homeless, sometimes staying on a couch and other times sleeping outside. He reported not being able to stay at the local shelter because they required him to be sober. The changing point occurred when his significant other who was also an alcoholic and he were living in a tent and she died from exposure to the elements in the middle of the winter. It wasn't until he was hospitalized for a month due to a serious injury that he was able to get sober. He has been able to build a program of recovery with strong involvement in Twelve Step meetings and counseling. He is volunteering at a homeless shelter providing support to others, especially during critical weather conditions.

Usually, we don't want to admit our patterns of powerlessness because that recognition is going to come with the stigma of a label of "alcoholic" or "addict." This prevents us from moving beyond the problem. Alcoholism and addiction, being chronic illnesses, are considered incurable because they only go into remission. Thus, we feel a sense of futility in that the diseases are never truly over. Since we interpret our problems as unique from others, we continue that sense of isolation that occurred during our addictions.

Admission to an addiction helps the person break through the confinement of their denial. To get to a destination that I want to go to I need to identify where I am starting out from. Hitting bottom is the usual terminology for acceptance of an addiction. We come to a moment of clarity where we can see the chaos that occurred in our addiction was necessary to seek help. This definitive state of awareness occurs based on the individual's life experience; some have to lose more than others.

When I was in a halfway house I had the same sobriety date as another friend who also lived in that recovery house. Pete and I celebrated our recovery/sobriety birthdays at a Twelve Step meeting, where we got our sobriety chip and a birthday cake. After two years sober, Pete went out one more time and drank, getting into a car accident that left him paralyzed from the neck down. A short time later, I heard from friends that he had come back into recovery, but I couldn't face him because I thought his physical injuries were more than I could bear. However, I ran into him at a recovery event about one year later and he looked at me and said, "I know why you haven't come to see me." He said, 'I want you to know that this accident opened my eyes so I could gain what this program of recovery could truly be for me.' We sometimes think that this is the worst bottom that can occur for ourselves, when perhaps it's all we can endure.

The addict will show obsessive compulsion as a driving force and it becomes imbedded in our personality. If an addict is given a psychological profile test such as the MMPI (Minnesota Multiphasic Personality Inventory), in most cases it will show positive for obsessive compulsive personality. Once a person develops a personality trait such as this as an adult, it remains with us the rest of our adult lives. To the addict it simply means we work hard and play hard, yet we don't know how to establish limits for ourselves. This does not mean we don't get better, it simply is an adjustment. Addicts are driven people, and using the resources of the obsessive compulsive personality becomes the driving force for our recovery to begin. We simply are applying a purpose and direction to the energy we already have.

Often we are our own worst critics and our own biggest obstacles in dealing with a problem in our lives. Once we get beyond this barrier of self and start building relationships with others who can help us find a solution, things get better. One of the purposes of the First Step is to bring the problems that have occurred because of our addictions to the surface. Embarrassment is an emotion that often prevents us from sharing our problems with others. When a person gets a DUI and his name is printed in the newspaper, he experiences that embarrassment and will avoid talking about what caused it. When there are a series of consequences as a result of abuse, it triggers the feeling of shame, which only increases the sensitivity to how others perceive us.

Shame is an internalized emotional reaction that tells us our value has lessened (that because of our actions we are not enough). So we hide. This avoidance of involvement with others keeps us from talking about things that trigger negative feelings about ourselves, but it impedes any progress.

Denial becomes a prison holding us locked in behind its' bars. We denied we had a problem in-spite of all the evidence to the contrary. We lied to ourselves, believing that the reason for our problems was not our own doing. Riding the wave of denial kept our temporary solution to our problems available to us, our addiction.

All of our survival defenses hold us back from confronting an addiction. The confronting of our lifestyle surrounding addiction ends that lifestyle and begins another. Although there may be intense pain surrounding an addiction, it still is a lifestyle that the person has become accustomed to. To begin a new journey without the addiction is uncharted territory. The brain functioning process in changing our thinking patterns can begin to take root in about a ninety day period of time. Twelve Step programs suggest, for in the beginning of recovery to attend ninety meetings in ninety days.

The premise of the Twelve Steps is to integrate us back into healthy relationships with others through the term "We" at the beginning of the First Step. This concept of being part of a mutual effort as a group of people is the beginning of regaining an equal concept of self in relationship to others.

This injection of involvement takes the person out of the potential sabotaging elements of their lifestyle. The term hitting bottom is well recognized by a person coming to terms with alcoholism or addictions. Starting to write out a First Step brings these issues to the surface. Often when beginning recovery and starting to share our First Step with others, we will have a burden of negative emotions that have been built up. When we are processing these emotions which we have held in for so long, we respond with remorse, anger, guilt, shame and other negative emotions. The task at hand is to come to terms with our own reflection that has been hidden from view of others and ourselves. This emotional experience echoes to us how empty the experience of addictions has been. This moment of clarity is the fire that drives the recovering addict.

Simply saying your name and that you're an alcoholic or addict at a Twelve Step meeting can be a large step towards acceptance of the First Step. When a person shares this about themselves at a meeting, their peers recognize them as a colleague in recovery. This opens the door for building relationships with peers, almost like a rite of passage. Often I have heard people at meetings say that this is the most expensive club they ever belonged to, because of the financial, pain and suffering it cost to get there. The more we share about our addiction at a meeting, the more aware we become of our problem. Meetings on the First Step, in which the group is discussing, give us an opportunity to gain more of a realization of how this Step pertains to us.

The First Step brings these circumstances to the surface by writing about them and sharing them with others. By doing so, denial becomes replaced with awareness, as it has impeded our vision. Yes it brings to the surface a lot of pain that we have kept buried beneath the surface, but by exposing it to light it transforms into personal motivation to sustain recovery. We experience a moment of clarity which brings us one step further into recovery. So if we are saying pain is the motivator for change, then the amount of personal pain experienced to make change needs to be determined by the individual.

Writing-out and sharing a First Step is a powerful experience which ignites the motivation and inspiration to halt an addiction. It is necessary for us to acknowledge where we have been in order to chart a new course of action. This is the first step to recovery from addictions.

Writing out patterns of powerlessness is the first part of this Step. Using a First Step guide to write out our self-assessment is recommended to take a thorough view of this Step. It is looking at the specific actions, which for us demonstrate patterns of loss of control in our use of the substance or compulsive behavior. Some examples are: The inability to predict when we would stop, our intention was to go out for a few hours to a bar with some friends which turns into the whole day; We switched from one addiction to another substance or addictive behavior such as gambling, and ended up with our lives going out of control again; We swore we would never drink and drive again and got a second DUI; We made commitments to stop our substance or addictive behavior to loved ones and hid our use from them to avoid their anger.

The second part of the First Step is unmanageability, due to our addictions. We continue to write the circumstances of our personal actions which demonstrate this unmanageability. There are two areas we look at. The first is the external unmanageability and what impact it had on our lives: legal issues, family problems, loss of relationships, financial, loss of jobs, emotional and physical consequences, and sexuality. In our disease of dependency our actions or lack of actions had a devastating effect on ourselves, family and those who shared our lives.

The second part of the unmanageability Step is identifying and admitting our internal denial system that kept our addictions continuing. There were certain core beliefs that supported us to continue to defend our actions. For instance, in the offender role, we may have felt deserving and self-entitlement in our abuse of substances or other addictive behaviors. This created a false self-image that their rights and needs are more important than others. We may have blamed others or past events for our actions, keeping us locked into our addictions. An individual in the victim role feels imprisoned. Victim patterns are created either because of a relationship with an offender, locked behind their high expectations for themselves; or due to losses, mental illness, trauma or chronic pain. Their focus is that they are not enough in their present circumstances and lack the ability to change. The person in an isolating/ hidden role is a master of deception. Often I have heard people describe their reasoning for this was either feeling self-entitled and didn't need to change, or feeling not enough to change. All of these behaviors keep the person isolated from others so that they don't interfere with their practice of their addictions.

These internal justifications for our actions placed us in an imbalance in our relationships with others. We need to identify which dominant trait followed our addictions, or more than one: victim, offender or isolating behaviors. The purpose of this is that these patterns need to be recognized and addressed for freedom from addictions to take hold. By recognizing this trait we continue to build unconditional relationships with others while working the Steps.

I have seen hundreds of people share their First Step, and at the end they experience a release that allows them the freedom to pursue another path. First Steps usually are written in an autobiographical manner and include sharing the personal experiences which led to the patterns of loss of control they had with the substance, and then the unmanageability of their life which followed. There are many different types of First Step guides available to help accomplish this task. "Narcotics Anonymous" and "Hazelden Publications" have resources. Online resources are available through search engines, also. Just look for "Twelve Step workbooks and worksheets". The authors of this book have created a website with downloadable resources which we have collected for this reason at: www.12StepsUnlocked.com.

After writing out this First Step process with guidance from a sponsor or a counselor, the best thing to do is present the information to your sponsor, a mentor of some kind, or a group. Treatment groups that are Twelve Step-based will usually have a person present a First Step on their substance abuse, as part of the treatment program. There is Twelve Step meetings set up in a series of group discussions to assist people processing the Step. A Christian support group called "Celebrate Recovery" uses a Step workbook that follows their members' Christian beliefs and interpretations. "Back to Basics" is another Twelve Step meeting offering the alcoholic the ability to work through the Steps in a series of four meetings. There are NA workbooks to assist people in sharing the Step, and in some cases counselors have helped people with it in individual sessions.

What this whole process does is help break through some of the denial that is still in our life, and brings into context just how much it damaged our personal relationships with others. As a result, the information shared with others is placed in the forefront of our mind, literally. The awareness of our problem comes to the surface in the present. Our conscious experience in making decisions is made in the cerebral cortex, in the frontal lobe of the brain. This literally brings the information to the forefront of our minds. What this action does is make the information in our consciousness known as a priority in our immediate goals and expectations of our behavior.

Addictions become part of a compulsive action. It no longer takes a conscious decision to act on our addictions. We are accustomed to our actions and we become less aware of them, that's part of being in a rut or a cycle that has been going on for a long time. This automatic reaction to acting out in our addictions also blocks our internal value system to evaluate our actions. We go on automatic pilot following a path that seems to bring us back in a full circle.

I remember meditating in front of a new candle I had gotten as a gift. The outer layer of the candle appeared to be a woven framework around the wick forming a globe around it and leaving small openings to see the flickering light. I sat calmly and observed the candle and I began to interpret it as being like an addiction. If in my addictions I was like the candle, my addictions would reflect my spiritual light and magnify it. As I put more resources into my addiction, like the outer layer of the candle it would continue to grow around my inner light. When there was no more oxygen left, it would snuff out the light within. We interpret that addictions are creating positive energy in our life, like the reflective light of the candle. We continue to use more of the substance, and give more power to our addiction. Because we are giving it other resources in our life it begins to grow, surrounding us. Slowly, addiction uses up all of our resources until it extinguishes the light within us.

The self-disclosure in sharing our First Step with others in recovery is the key to laying out the building blocks of our new lifestyle, without addiction. This action demands honesty about the circumstances of our addiction and sharing it with others. This subsequently helps to gain self-acceptance of our actions and paves the way for personal accountability. Through our collective experience in working the First Step with others, we find comfort in being released from the isolation of our addictions. By sharing with others who have suffered from their addictions, we hear our story portrayed in their experience. We hear in the meetings, 'I can't, but we can.'

I had a client who was involved in counseling with me continue for one year of individual sessions as part of his aftercare plan. He went over his First Step with me, which he originally had done in the first couple months of recovery. He then processed another First Step at the end of one year in recovery. He stated he was 'more of an alcoholic a year sober than when he first came into recovery'. He reported that he was more aware at that point in time that he is an alcoholic, than when he first came in. His denial had subsided where he could see more clearly after a longer period of recovery.

Because addictions are a chronic disease, they have the ability to go into remission, offering the individual a daily reprieve from their compulsion. Because of the power addiction has in our lives, it may weave back in through other back doors. A person may have been addicted to alcohol and then because of chronic pain, slip back into addiction through use of narcotics. Or, a person may switch into behavioral addictions such as sex addiction or gambling addiction. Anytime I begin to use something to change how I feel, I should review it with the First Step.

The Twelve Step program is the individual's insurance policy to keep them from going down the road into another type of addiction, or relapse into their old ones. The challenges in the road to recovery we walk can be difficult at times. The pain of living can occur long after we have stopped using due to circumstances that were either the aftermath of our addictions in lost relationships; or due to pain that derived from other natural losses which is part of our sober living experience. These life experiences may seem to bring chaos back into our lives. We may find ourselves acting out compulsions that we had not encountered as a problem in the past. Fear is the basis for most of our character defects, which triggers us into further victim and offender patterns in our lives. Yes, our addictions were a symptom of the problem that blocked us from successful, meaningful relationships with others. The underlying factors that contributed to our addictions haven't left just because we stopped using, but may remain in remission by working the Twelve Steps. Using the First Step at different times, in coming to terms with ongoing life experiences, causes us to return for further inventory of our lives.

Recovery is known as the gift that you have to work for. Through our continued experience in building relationships with others in recovery, we meet the challenges that come up on a daily basis. We are now ready to move onto Step Two.

Step Two

Came to believe that a Power greater than ourselves could restore us to sanity.

After completion of the First Step, people have come to an understanding that by their own admission, they don't have the answers that will help them work through their addiction. Part of the addictive personality that I have found to be true of the addict is self-reliance and they don't like to ask for help from anybody.

Addictions compel people to become more isolated and anti-social in their interactions with others. They may be charismatic and outgoing, but the true nature of their intimate feelings is something they choose not to share. We tried within our own power to find a resolution to the problems in our lives and no solutions were revealed to us. The concept of trusting something outside of us had to be realized for the answers to become available to us. Our failure turns us to try the one thing we avoid using the most: trust in our relationships with others in recovery.

Step Two takes people to the next task at hand in building trust in their relationships with the outside world. It prepares them to embark on this journey to trust someone or something outside of themselves in order to break through the chaos and isolation of addiction. This, simply put, is the Second Step: becoming part of something greater than ourselves. I believe the word "greater," in this context, means that my life is in transition through my thoughts and experiences on a daily basis. If I am able to incorporate others' experiences into something new, then my life transitions into something greater, or different.

Starting at Step Two, and continuing through Step Nine, there is a two-phase process going through Steps Two and Three, Steps Four and Five, and so on. The beginning Step is preparation which builds awareness, and creates an attitude of willingness and being teachable. This position of humility opens the doorway which allows the person to access other resources. This fuels the drive to move onto the next Step. The following Step is an action Step of change. In making changes in ourselves we rely upon the support and resources of others and our Higher Power to accomplish the task at hand.

One definition of humility I've seen in the Webster Dictionary is 'gaining insight into limitations and assets'. I believe that people who suffer from addictions have a personal, social and spiritual dilemma in feeling part of the world around them. They use an addiction to fill in the gaps.

We must break through the barriers that our addictions have placed in our lives through denial. To achieve this we have to gain the ability to be rendered helpless. In some cases, a drowning person who is aggressively splashing around has to be knocked unconscious so that the rescuer has the ability to save them.

There is an old saying that "there are no atheists in foxholes." Motivation for change in our beliefs occurs when what worked before is no longer working in our lives. Are people being compliant because they have to? The answer is usually "yes".

There is an old story about someone standing on the edge of a cliff and the earth gives away under his feet. He falls and grasps onto a root that is sticking out of the side of the cliff. There he hangs, with no way to climb back up and certain death if he lets go. He struggles and feels himself begin to weaken. He then asks if there is a God, and promises that if He helps him out of this dilemma that he will never doubt Him again. A voice from afar says "let go of the root." Of course before he takes this advice, the climber probably would ask "is there anyone else up there?" Asking for help is the demonstration of working the Second Step.

Addicts need to have people as sounding boards to their spiritual needs. It is essential to the healing process. They may not yet feel equal to others, but that doesn't stop them from being teachable. As they change while working the Second Step, they are opened up to view the world in a much different way. I often had clients who had begun attending Twelve Step meetings years before, but they were not open to what the meetings had to offer. This time around, they would say the meetings appeared to have changed and there were a lot more interesting things being said, even the people had more to offer them. The truth is it didn't have anything to do with the other people at the meetings. It was they who had experienced change in themselves which lead to their different perception of others. The recovering person is one who has to let go of negative viewing, or filters, and become open to possibilities of change in their life.

The term "came to believe" sets the stage for letting go of the control we have exhibited through our character defects which acted as a wall, hindering the flow of energy and resources from others and our Higher Power. Once we have let go of all reservations and have come to an understanding, we become totally vulnerable. I use the concept of a trapeze artist who must jump from one trapeze bar to the next. It is blind faith that the person in recovery has to grasp onto.

When I was in treatment for addiction I was in a long-term residential program (therapeutic community). Those programs back thirty-seven years ago were aggressive and sometimes brutal in their methods. When I first arrived I thought, "oh, looks like I moved back home". I was a fighter in spirit and was in a group therapy session where they were pounding on me verbally for three hours. I was about to break emotionally. I could no longer hold onto my control. Instead, very manipulatively, I told them I had to be excused from group right then because I was the cook and I needed to be putting dinner on if they wanted anything to eat for lunch that day. They let me go and I went downstairs to put lunch on. At that time, I had decided to commit suicide. I knew if the group pushed any further that I would break down. But from my addictions, I felt I had one piece of dignity left and if I let it out, all they would do was step on it and squash what was left of me. So I took a large kitchen knife and went to the top of a tall stairway to the basement next to the kitchen and placed the point just below my ribs and started to fall forward. A peer from the group came down, sensing something was wrong with me. He grabbed me and we both almost went down the stairs. I went back to the group and broke down for the first time. The interesting thing was that they didn't step on me. They just listened to the pain that was way deep inside. I believe that, for me, was the beginning of taking the Second Step. It was moving to ask for help from others, without any reservations. It is trusting in someone or something outside of themselves which is necessary for their survival. I can equate this to if we need surgery, we must trust the Anesthesiologist, Doctor and staff to watch out for us and maintain medical support during a time, putting our life in their hands. Step Two is the beginning of building trust in relationships outside of ourselves, through taking the initiative in asking for help from others. They begin the process of being teachable in interactions with others. Resources can come in the form of counselors, treatment centers, clergy, churches and Twelve Step support systems, and it certainly is a benefit to search out one's concept of a Higher Power. This is an opportunity to be open to all information available to us. Getting a sponsor is another way of practicing the Second Step. Reading Twelve Step literature and inspirational materials can help the individual in recovery, as well as attending Twelve Step workshops and conventions with others. These are physical aspects of working the Second Step and remaining teachable.

The term "restore us to sanity" is a reflection of the chaos which addictions flooded into our lives. We may have been aware of the condition, but we were incapable of doing anything about it. Our perception of the world around us was fear based. We saw it being a hostile environment which warranted not being trusted. We used control to maintain intimate relationships because, in some ways, we perceived we didn't have an inherent right to have them. Some of us are dominant figures in relationships with our partner or family members. Others of us take on a passive role in our most intimate relationships. This route is a perceived sense of control by saying, "it is my fault. I have paid the price to be in an intimate relationship." These are conditional relationships rather than healthy, unconditional relationships which sustain our emotional and spiritual well-being.

Most of us were incapable of being truly humble in our addictions. This can be seen by the fact that we used our addictions to change how we felt rather than our relationships with others. In the light of recovery we can use the resources of being teachable and open minded to allow other resources to sift into our lives. In some cases, as in the isolator, we moved through the motions of life disassociating ourselves from others and not allowing anyone to touch us emotionally. Either way we remained isolated and alone. We refused to face the reality of our own making. We continued to do the same things, always expecting different results; or we tried different things, always expecting the same result, expecting them not to work. It was the continued use of the substance in our addiction that kept our world from crumbling.

We used the substance to change how we felt but it was only a temporary solution. In viewing our lives at this point, it cannot be denied that our lives need restoring, and a total overhaul of our relationships with others. This restoration process is a lifelong process, keeping in balance a reasonable set of expectations that is acceptable by our standards and others.

We begin to experience success in this restoration, that we have stopped our addiction process. Days turn to weeks and weeks turn to months. The challenges of the Second Step continue to surface. However, we build relationships in recovery with not only the fellowship in Twelve Step programs, but with our families and loved ones.

Developing hope is a process of seeing the outcome of our actions which changes our view of the future. We kindle hope by seeing others at Twelve Step meetings achieve recovery. We begin to believe that the principals of recovery in the Twelve Steps could be construed as a Power greater than ourselves. These concepts are tools and when these principals are put into action through people's lives, we see the vision of possibilities form in our lives and others. We experience the power of the group and get reassurance of what the program promises-through a hug from someone, or at the closing of a meeting when people say "Keep coming back, it works if you work it."

Opening our minds to the possibility of there being power outside of us is a concept that can sometimes trigger fear in people's lives. First of all the substance we were using was a power greater than our-selves in that it altered our values and how we conducted ourselves in our relationships with others. Addictions are a negative force of power, greater than our-selves, which causes personal destruction. The effort to build a program of recovery through a positive force of healing and through the combined efforts of others brings out the best in us thereby empowering ourselves.

This Step suggests we find a Higher Power, being a loving God, or group of principals or resources that guides us in our recovery. Whatever concept we find and rely on as that resource or combined resources, we begin to work the Step. It has been my experience that an individual who is growing spiritually has a concept of a Higher Power that will change as their life changes. Often we will question our sponsor and others in recovery as to how they see their Higher Power and what their inspiration for recovery is. We may become students of spiritual materials we read. We may integrate parts of what someone else uses and merge it with our own beliefs. As we find elements that fit for us, we begin to develop a set of beliefs. These beliefs help to build a sense of confidence as we see them working in our lives. By seeing from our personal experience how these concepts fit in our life, we build faith. As our concept of a Higher Power develops, this concept gives us reassurance in this new found direction in our life. It is recognized in Twelve Step recovery that everyone has the right to their own concept of a Higher Power.

The attitude of being teachable is at the core of the Second Step. While applying the principles in developing our relationships with others in the program, we listen to others and absorb as much as we can of what the program is about. We get this from the fellowship of Twelve Step programs, the meetings and our sponsor. We create the attitude of being teachable by asking for help from others and listening.

Often people have said "fake it until you make it". You may not have a Higher Power but, by trying the concepts on and practicing them, eventually outcomes present themselves in helping to develop your own beliefs. Prayer is a positive element of opening up to the concepts of a Higher Power, not to be confused with religion. It is a resource that has been reported successful for many people in recovery. Calling your Higher Power by name, or Him or Her is up to the person. Faith is applying the principles of trusting something outside of us that we don't understand. We can only learn by trying things out. If they don't fit, we can discard them afterward. Give them an honest chance to work first. Prayer assists us in creating an attitude of being teachable in our lives.

There are Second Step guides that can help people write out the ways they are taking measures in finding and building a relationship with a Power greater than themselves. The spiritual side of the Step is absolutely a positive part of the recovery process. Finding a Higher Power that works for you is part of this process. I have been a student of religions for many years and am not going to impose my beliefs onto the reader. This Step opens the door to the individual developing a personal relationship with a Power outside of himself or herself.

Some people have reported using the term G.O.D. (Good Orderly Direction). Being open to the concepts of spirituality is part of the task at hand. Attending church, talking to clergy or ministers or asking others what works for them can be helpful in accomplishing this Step.

I once came back from a Twelve Step Agape weekend conference with a friend of mine who was a devout Christian. We were talking about the Bible saying that there were two billion angels on Earth, and he said to me that they could be anyone or anywhere around us. At that moment, we came up to a "T" in the road and a stop sign. A truck drove by and the driver said, "Hi, boys." The imagery of the situation at hand struck us both and we began to laugh.

Another time, I was at an Indian restaurant in Minneapolis and a professional street preacher and the restaurant manager, who was Buddhist, were having a debate over their different beliefs. Once the manager noticed there were patrons lining up, he shook the man's hand, thanked him and said, "I hope your faith is as strong as mine."

Having the sense that we are not alone in our relationships with others or in our spiritual relationship makes life in recovery more meaningful. Most of us pray at times in our lives and those who are religious or spiritual in their beliefs do believe that the God of their understanding speaks through their relationships with others. When I did a resident internship at a state hospital there were Schizophrenic patients who reported getting their answers directly from God.

When I was sober a few years and living in South Minneapolis, I shared an apartment with a roommate who spent a lot of time at his girlfriend's place. All alone one night before I went to sleep, as usual, I was saying the Eleventh Step prayer, asking for knowledge of God's will for me and the power to carry that out. At that second, my roommate stuck his head in the room and said, "Hello." Not knowing anyone was there but God listening to my prayers, I screamed at the top of my lungs. It was so loud that it made him scream. Mine was the same reaction that John Denver had in the movie, "Oh, God," when George Burns appeared as God. What I am saying here is that our efforts to find a Higher Power are not going to magically relieve us of our addictions, but will give us the tools to work through them.

The miracle that we are looking for may not be walking on water, but the miracle is living without addictions one day at a time. Our relationships with others are the foundation for building recovery. There are no burning bushes that will magically take our problems away or delete our painful character defects. We are given the tools and it is up to us, with direction and support, to achieve our goals.

We keep with our efforts to continue in recovery by being willing to follow direction, and accepting the natural outcome of our actions. These are principals that are part of recovery, through acceptance of our part in our relationships with others. We may find circumstances in our lives that don't seem fair to us. We must be open to the concepts that the program teaches us about recovery, offering us a different perspective of the problem. We work the program by going to meetings, asking for help and working the Steps.

The other aspect of our lives which we need to watch out for is the rekindling of our pride and control, and allowing them back in our lives again. In the process of getting recovery, someone may think "I got it" and stop doing the things that allowed them to be teachable. This would usually trigger their old character defects of creating conditional relationships with others, using control to try to benefit them or to go back to a way that seemed familiar to them. This triggers further isolation. The reference of being teachable is in believing that we are in the process of recovery, "getting it". Sometimes when I say "I got it", I probably already lost it and have to work at finding it again.

Once we have gotten to this point, we are in the attitude of change described through the Second Step. We are now listening. Thus, we move onto the Third Step.

Step Three

Made a decision to turn our will and our lives over to the care of God, as we understood Him.

Hope was the attitude created through the process of Step Two through making the effort to ask for help from others. Step Three takes the individual to the next natural place of action, the second phase of humility, that of being able to receive help from others. Step Two was preparation in developing the attitude of coming to believe in something greater than ourselves. Step Three is the demonstration of our actions in building relationships, both with others and our Higher Power. This Step is essential for building a long lasting connection with others and our Higher Power.

It is natural to have some fear of what the outcome may be if I pursue this Step. We know by now that change is happening in ourselves and in our relationships with others, but who are we becoming? Change is inevitable in life, and our expectations of ourselves change based on our changing needs. We are transforming ourselves as we speak. Every cell in our body changes and is replaced, physically we are not in the same body throughout our life. The essence, of who we are, our consciousness, is still the same. We step forward by taking this Step to initiate change in our life rather than in the past waiting for someone else to make the effort.

Carrying the load of our life experience without the connection and reassurance of others has been the burden of addiction. That isolation is broken like a drop of water joining into a beautiful lake. We start this journey by saying the words and then our actions demonstrate our commitment to change. This is a Step of action that unfolds beneath our feet leaving footprints, showing us that we are on a new path. This revelation of change redefines who we are becoming. We leave behind the chaos of control in everything around our lives and step forward into our unknown potential. Turning our life over to something we don't understand is a difficult task, we don't know what the outcome will be. We take the opposite physical reactions instead of being tense and withholding, we relax and let go.

We need to take action, so we set goals going to school, getting a job and we put forth the initiative which our Higher Power instills in us with motivations and spiritual fitness. There will be setbacks, all of us have doubt. Even Mother Teresa doubted her faith in her memoirs. We pick ourselves up and try again. We put forth the effort to live in a manner that the spiritual principals present: honesty, hope, trust, forgiveness and faith. The Third Step is to be applied to all areas of our lives. We can hold back on reservations thinking that we can still control our relationship and our work environment. These beliefs were part of our old denial system. We set conditional relationships with others based on our control needs. Letting go of the diet that left us malnourished, emotionally and spiritually, is necessary. We can't make a great cake unless we follow the recipe.

So the Third Step can be defined as the integration of self in all facets of the world around me, the physical, emotional, social and spiritual elements of the world. Each experience I go through in coming into balance with those around me is the action part of the Third Step.

I was troubled when I saw a psychologist present at a lecture on the recovery community. He was interpreting Twelve Step recovery as a subculture that had a set of beliefs that were better than the beliefs from the rest of society. Later, however, I talked with my old sponsor, Bill M., who was one of the earlier members (old timers) of Alcoholics Anonymous. He said that the Twelve Steps are to help people to become part of society, not to create a new one.

That made a lot of sense to me. Simply going to Twelve Step meetings is part of the physical aspects of working the Third Step. How we interact in the world is started by finding a place to experience these new values and testing them out with others in Twelve Step meetings. This fellowship makes us more confident with our new values before we take them out into the world around us.

For example, I remember going to meetings and what would stick out in my mind was a conflict I had with what another member of the meeting said. I would not remember anything good about the meeting. I brought this up to my sponsor at that time. I took his advice and began to look at the similarities rather than the differences in what people were saying at the meetings. In doing so, I discovered I was afraid I would lose my focus of individuality if I came to a place of acceptance in the program rather than continue to be an antagonist there. I didn't want to become a selfless drone. Then I realized it was my actions that were creating my reality before it actually occurred in my life. I was allowing pessimism and negativity to define who others were and that caused me to be left alone.

It isn't a perfect process which this program unfolds, but it will do as who we are becoming today. Tomorrow my views on things may change. I have gone to Twelve Step meetings and had conflict with what some people were saying, but through processing I found out later that I actually agreed with their views. Other times I have heard someone share their story and it brought a feeling of personal acceptance and empathy.

I remember being uncomfortable about dancing unless I was high on something, so I only went dancing with others who were also young in recovery. Part of recovery is learning from others who have gone through the process, mentors and sponsors in recovery, but it is also essential to have that peer group who are going through the same process we are. It helps keep us aware that we are not alone anymore. I was in a group of people who were in the first few years of recovery and we were getting retrained, going to college and building new lives for ourselves. That ability to share our experiences with a group in recovery is immeasurable. Going to a workshop or going back to school and opening oneself up to new ideas and expressions is also part of the Third Step.

My first sponsors in Narcotics Anonymous and in Alcoholics Anonymous worked the Steps with me, teaching me from different perspectives. My sponsor in AA, Bill M., went through the Steps in the time honored fashion that was shown to him. He was an old-timer, getting sober in Akron, Ohio. My other sponsor in Narcotics Anonymous, Steve P., shared his experience, being of similar age and lifestyle in our addictions. Both sponsors offered me strengths that assisted me in building a strong foundation in recovery. This experience was part of the Third Step because I was able to receive a part of my sponsors' experiences and make them part of my own.

Our character defects have disabled us in becoming part of something greater than ourselves. We must break through the barriers that have kept us isolated from the world and the God of our understanding. There are three patterns that exist in our character defects. A person will choose the form of behavior that gives them a sense of control. The first being the offender, through our self-entitlement, "I'll take it if I want it" attitude; this jeopardizes our ability to build humility in our lives because we sustain control. The second is the victim character defect in "not feeling worthy of"; we believe we lack the ability to break through the barriers that block our connection with a loving God of our understanding and how He unfolds in our life. The third pattern is the isolator. This pattern is used to avoid conflict, which is like a double edged sword because it deprives us of the ability to develop intimacy in relationships.

In the offender traits, self-entitlement develops as we become more isolated from others as a result of our addictions. Dwelling in that isolation, we become focused on our personal needs and gratification. We become self-centered in filling our needs, and numb to the needs of others through our offender traits. The old adage is 'I want what I want when I want it'. This lack of continuity creates a shield from seeing the possibility of a Higher Power working in our life. In this scenario, they have become the God in their life. This person needs to be released from their grandiosity to see the true picture of the world and themselves. By breaking this cycle the person develops an understanding of a God consciousness that is the center of the universe, not them.

At a treatment program where I was clinical director, we admitted a lot of young men who came mostly from wealthy families. The patterns of use for many of these clients were based on self-entitlement issues. As part of their treatment, I had them volunteer for twenty hours a week at a volunteer agency in the community. This gave them the opportunity to give to others unconditionally and come into balance in their life. By adding this new perspective, they began developing empathy and sensitivity to others.

In the victim traits the isolation becomes a prison, keeping our pain contained while only being able to focus on our survival. The victim seeks approval from their offender to find safety. The benefit of their situation is that they don't have to make major life decisions because they are made for them. The lack of nurturing support from their partner leaves them feeling like an empty vessel. The other aspect of the victim of circumstance is the physical or emotional pain of their losses becoming the center of their world. Their search for relief turns into an obsession to temporarily numb their pain. The victim may feel abandoned by their God, because He didn't protect them from their abuse, physical pain, or loss. The victim then contained their pain in silence in order to survive; their offender becomes their higher power. The key here is working through distrust and breaking the silence of their pain. To do this they must share it with others and build trust in a loving, attentive God of their understanding.

In the isolator traits, this person may use intelligence and logic to sustain a perception of control in their life. This person uses isolation by sometimes saying "I'll do it myself". It becomes another barrier that blocks their ability to perceive a loving God of their understanding. It is a self-protective defense that the person uses to feel safe in their world. The person has to build a sense of safety in their new relationships before taking the risk to share with others. They begin this process by attending Twelve Step meetings regularly, getting accustomed to their new found support system. Once that process occurs the person begins the natural process of self-disclosure and listening to others, building intimacy in these relationships. Instead of working from the inside out by analyzing it to death, they must jump in with both feet. It is like trying on a new style of clothes which we are not accustomed to. Once the initial risk has been accomplished they begin to build relationships in recovery. It is an act of vulnerability that we experience when we let go of our outer shell of isolation through our character defects. The person builds confidence in relationships with others and a loving God, which replaces their world of isolation. Relieving a person of a major character defect takes the person out of their comfort zone so they may experience a different perspective of the world in which they are not in control.

Another example is when I had a woman come into a clinic where I was working. She had been in multiple treatment programs groomed for wealthy individuals, and treatment never took. I recommended that she be referred to a program in another State, where her female peers were low income individuals. She came back three years later to a treatment facility where I worked and talked with me. She had remained sober for the past two years and was enrolled in an internship at a prestigious facility to become a counselor. She stated that the motive for my referral was either brilliant or crazy, and asked which it was? I told her that perception must be up to her.

Doing service work is a physical action we can take as part of the Third Step process because it is getting us involved and making us part of the Twelve Step meetings. It can be as simple as putting the coffee on or collecting the donations at a Twelve Step meeting. You can be a greeter or lead secretary, or just attend a business meeting. I overcame my shyness by starting a Twelve Step meeting where there wasn't one and then spent time going out and telling others where it was. Attending and participating in Twelve Step meetings is part of the Third Step because you are taking an action, which is helping you become part of something that is bigger than yourself.

When we attempt a new behavior we still have our previous perceptions of what the outcome will be. As a result of our new actions we formulate a new opinion on how that behavior benefited us.

I remember being invited to a recovery party for the first time, and was regretting going because I thought I would be bored and there would just be a lot of people sitting around, doing nothing but staring at one another. Instead, I ended up staying until late in the evening, playing games and having exciting, fun conversations. I wondered the next day why I had thought I was going to have a boring time, and then I realized that I was drawing from my prior experience of parties where I and others were intoxicated.

Attending a church that represents your beliefs also could be part of the Third Step. Many of us have had adverse experiences in our religious training, feeling that we were subjected to these beliefs which we may not have believed were our own. If our negative feelings about religion are too strong, we may need to examine all of our feelings about our spirituality, both negative and positive. We may have to take time to review our feelings, if we felt beliefs imposed on us, and talk with our sponsor or other spiritual advisors. It may require us to begin with a simpler concept of a Higher Power. Some people use the Twelve Steps and the principles of the program as their Higher Power. This allows an opportunity for them to build upon their philosophical and spiritual beliefs.

Agnostics, not knowing the character of God but believing there is something out there, often show up in recovery. If we are at a place in our lives to rejuvenate a feeling of inspiration that we had earlier experienced, it could be a good thing to take a risk by attending a service from our religious upbringing; or, it may be time to change our spiritual beliefs to attempt to build upon a new understanding of God as we see Him. I perceive myself as a student of religion and feel that I must practice spirituality in my life. Many of us have reservations about buying into organized religion, but most of us believe in spirituality of some sort.

For years I presented a lecture on organized religion and spirituality to treatment centers and outside community resources. Religion gives us an organized process that helps many to build a relationship with a God of their understanding. What I noticed was that some felt conflicted in their experience with religion, but almost all felt positive about concepts of spirituality. Yes, religion isn't perfect, but it does serve as a unifying resource for large parts of our society.

The Third Step, being an action Step, uses the term, "… turn our will and our lives over to the care of God as we understood Him." So how do we perform these actions and what is the correct path for us? The Third Step says not to worry: 'It is of our understanding,' so that means what we do should be a natural action that feels comfortable for us. We build upon what we are doing spiritually at that point in our lives for that Third Step challenge.

I had a friend in recovery who was a scientist. He reported that he began his concept of a Higher Power by believing that Duke Ellington was that entity for him. Very sincerely, he told me that Ellington's music helped to uplift his spirit and change how he felt. While music may seem to us as only recreational, it definitely can change how we feel. Of course, music was just the beginning of changes in his beliefs. In fact, it was the start of a course of action that led him to become a counselor and he then helped start a national council for addictions for African Americans. His actions on his Third Step in life helped him transcend and become more than what he was.

I believe prayer and meditation are necessary forms of communication that serve our ability to express our most intimate spiritual needs. These are important parts of keeping our focus on recovery as a spiritual journey. Prayer assists us to humble ourselves not just to ask for a direction in our lives, but also to open ourselves up to the attitudes and willingness for change to occur. One method known is the Third Step prayer, "God I offer myself to thee—to build with me and to do with me as Thou wilt. Relieve me of the bondage of self, that I may better do Thy will always!" From Big Book of Alcoholics Anonymous, How It Works, pages 63. © A.A. World Services, Inc. Reprinted with the permission of A.A. World Services, Inc. This prayer opens the door to loosening the grips of our character defects that plagued us through sustained self-will. Prayer induces an attitude of willingness and teachability. Another example is the Eleventh Step prayer, "praying for knowledge of God's will for us and the power to carry that out." This opens us up to a positive aspect of facilitating change. Our relationships with other people simply become tools which our Higher Power is giving us to assist us in this change.

Meditation is a process of bringing our consciousness and awareness in the present moment to facilitate the changes necessary in the here and now. Meditation stills our minds and approves our concentration to stay in the present. What type of meditation a person practices is up to the individual. Taking time out daily for prayer and meditation does not have to mean a significant amount of time. This activity can simply be reading a page from a daily meditation book and reflecting on it. Another way could be by reviewing our commitment to recovery and asking our Higher Power for guidance, with a few minutes of silence following.

Taking care of ourselves also is part of the Third Step. Yes, that's right: getting outside resources to improve our physical condition is going to change our attitude about the world we live in. This is our relationship with our-selves in taking care of our physical body. Taking care of our dental needs is a sign that we are feeling better about ourselves. We smile a lot more if we take care of our smiles. Physically taking care of our bodies through exercise and eating healthy foods helps give us the vitality we need; so does having a routine that is, in effect, a ritual. Often that includes working out at a gym with others, or just taking a walk in the neighborhood.

We look at self-indulgences through eating whatever we want, fast foods and sugar products. We read materials on self-care about nutrition and recognize self-defeating behaviors we have developed through poor eating habits. We begin to be aware of foods that we may be allergic to which can contribute to poor health. We review this through doing an inventory about our patterns. Through awareness and assistance we develop an eating and exercise plan that helps us bring balance in our personal lives. By doing these things, we begin to like ourselves and our bodies, thereby improving our health.

Taking better physical care of ourselves is a nurturing activity that triggers natural endorphins, and dopamine in the body. Forty minutes of aerobic exercise will trigger our metabolism to speed up for the next 36 hours. That's right. We have more energy and burn off more calories. It also triggers endorphins which give us a natural feeling of well-being. We can look up healthy eating plans over the Internet or talk with a nutritionist or doctor to educate ourselves on what helps our bodies, and what causes further damage, such as stress.

Often in early recovery we starve ourselves of needed sleep, sometimes because of surfacing issues triggering stress. During our sleep our bodies are restoring our health and repairing our bodies, so finding measures to insure adequate rest is a self-nurturing thing to do. Remember, feeling good inside offers us the ability to feel good about our surroundings.

Does your understanding of a loving God have a sense of humor? Life taken too seriously leaves a portion of the world untouched. I have found my lessons in life often have humor.

I had gotten married outside of Minneapolis, Minnesota. I rented a tuxedo for that weekend and planned to wear it on our short honeymoon at a bed and breakfast. I had forgotten to pay my snow removal parking tickets from the winter, which I usually did in the spring. As we were going on our honeymoon, police pulled me over for a tail light out. They saw that there was a warrant out for me because of my unpaid parking tickets and arrested me. My wife took the car back to her parents, but couldn't find me until the next morning. The police had taken me to another police precinct and on the way there they picked up someone else, a man dressed up in drag. In the police department they wanted to take police profile pictures of both of us together. I refused. They put me in a holding cell over night with the other man dressed in drag on my honeymoon night, and he wasn't even good looking.

Laughter is part of the Third Step and sharing it with others can bring us joy, and maybe even better health. Being sober and having a gut wrenching laugh is a healthy avenue for recovery. Having humor in our lives decreases stress and helps the circulation.

I had a long term friend in a Twelve Step program that developed Alzheimer's and I hadn't seen him for several because of his disease. I had gotten together with him with several other friends in recovery for dinner and while sitting and visiting with him he said, "Do you know me?" I said, "Yes, I've known you for years." He asked how long he was sober. I told him he was sober six years longer than me so he had --, years of sobriety. He said, 'You know I have Alzheimer's.' My response was asking him how he felt about that. He thought for a minute and said, 'Well, you know I came into this program screwed up, and I guess I will be leaving screwed up!'

Laughter not only decreases the drama in our lives, but it is a positive element that is socially acceptable and attractive to others. Letting out our sense of humor adds style to our sharing in relationships with others.

After a Twelve Step meeting one time, I spoke to a man who had bandages on his hip. He had just had surgery and reported having a type of cancer where they had to remove portions of his body. He said that his sponsor told him to stay sober even if his ass falls off. He looked at the bandages on his hip, and said well mine did, but I'm still sober!

In the process of recovery we see the potential possibilities in ourselves and in our relationships with others. We develop the skills to cope with the world around us. When we develop the attitude of sincerity in our belief in a Higher Power and have integrated it into our lives, we develop serenity.

I remember going to put on a meeting at a treatment center at a State Hospital. I was driving down the road and I felt like I was a contributing, healthy part of the world. I almost shuttered because I never felt that way before. That was my first experience in feeling serenity.

We notice a gradual change in our thinking becoming more positive. Our world view begins to change and we are no longer looking through glasses of denial, resentment and self-pity. We see the vast possibilities that are available to our lives. Our connection to the world is a spontaneous, fulfilling experience for ourselves and those we are involved with.

How am I taking action in Step Three to build unconditional relationships within the fellowship? This is a good place to build positive relationships. Once we have accomplished such relationships in Twelve Step fellowship we can integrate this process in our relationships with family and close friends. This may require getting outside counseling as part of the process. Family may not be interested in getting involved with any outside support system, but patience is recommended. We probably caused a lot of the wreckage which has caused them to withdraw from us. Building unconditional relationships is part of the Third Step because we have no control over the outcome. Losing the attitude of being controlling in our relationships gives us the flexibility to grow. We begin to establish trust and intimacy which was not there before. We begin to gather respect from others in demonstration of the consistency of our actions.

Finally, it is a good idea to start a Third Step inventory. It should review what actions we are taking which demonstrate letting go of self-will, trusting in a God of our understanding and how He unfolds in our life. It asks: what am I doing to practice the Third Step in all areas of my life which is affecting my physical, emotional, social and spiritual well-being? It is setting goals of actions which I intend to improve on, or I am initiating. How am I allowing myself to be a contributing part in my relationships with others? The result of actively taking this Step is that, for the first time in a long time, a person believes 'it's a brand new day and I'll be okay.' Now we are prepared to move onto Step Four.

Step Four

Made a searching and fearless moral inventory of ourselves.

When we moved on from Step Three, we proceeded to emerge as part of society again. In the reckoning of ourselves, we come to a place where we need to be aware of what impact our actions have had on others. Our substance abuse was the outside layer while the core of our addiction remained below the surface. We have to see the full impact that our addictions had on our lives. I stress the importance of doing Step Four, because without taking this Step an analogy might be buying a car with a faulty engine. What keeps our recovery working is gaining a clear perspective of what our life experience has created in our lives. When we look in a mirror the image we see is what we would like to believe about ourselves. A rigorously honest view of our actions gives us the tools that will sustain this new vehicle of recovery in our lives for years to come.

We become willing to bring light to the darkened halls of our past. We have hid in our addictions and pushed responsibility for our action back into the closets of our mind. We need to bring light to these experiences, through pen to paper.

The term "moral inventory" tends to scare people into thinking that they are being judged. It is simply an inventory of our character, both assets and liabilities. We are able to see through our review of this inventory that fear was the basis for most of our actions. We further realize that our perspective of control through our roles in conditional relationships caused harm not only to ourselves, but to those we loved most in our lives. We look at ways that we acted out as an offender, victim or through our absence or unavailability. In most cases we see these patterns early in life which continued through to the present.

The focus is on relationships, especially the impact our addictions had on our family. This is not to set blame, but to be aware of our actions. Some of our patterns of choice have given us power in relationships with others, other have taken it away. The effort of proceeding with this Step brings the person to grasp the core of their fears to the surface where they can be released.

Addicts tend to hold onto resentments which prolong the pain of these relationships in their lives. We make an inventory of our resentments. We look at relationships with family, employers, jails, institutions, religion, legal and people, places and things we hold resentments towards. We examine the entire circumstance that brought on the resentment and then identify our part. We begin to see similarities where we played out the victim, offender or isolator roles in our lives.

Our sexuality is another topic to address in this inventory. In the Big Book of Alcoholics Anonymous there was a reference for the need for the alcoholic to do a total sexual overhaul of their values in that area. That was a pretty big statement to make in the early 1930's. There was a reason for the authors at that time to recognize human sexuality being a significant issue to address in recovery. We have difficulty even talking about it without using some type of defensive humor, to cut through the insecurity. Perhaps it has to do with the fact that we, as humans, are prone to be monogamous, with one partner. The importance is sharing these sensitive needs with one individual, our partner. I once heard a presentation by Pat Carnes, who is a well-known Psychologist and has written several books on human sexuality. He presented that even a paraplegic can have a satisfied sense of their sexuality if they are able to communicate and receive their sexual needs from their partner, and provide for their partner's needs. So our sexuality and sexual needs can be fulfilled if we have the ability to communicate about them.

In order to communicate about these needs we must have three things in the relationship: trust, communication and intimacy. The three things which are lost in a relationship with an addict are trust, communication and intimacy. I am not saying that the practicing addict doesn't get their sexual needs met, but often they are not able to communicate about their sexual needs with their partner. Obviously alcoholics and addicts have had sex, so how do they communicate their needs? Often what happens is that one person becomes the provider for the sexual needs and the other is the receiver. In this way there is no need to discuss or make a decision about functioning in their sexual activity. Yes, women tend to more often be the provider for the needs of their partner's sexual needs in heterosexual relationships.

Often a lack of communication in our sexual relationship is recognized as a lack of foreplay. This absence of emotional contact with our partner triggers the need for some type of other arousal, often through fantasy. We then become stimulated from a sexual fantasy, sometimes even with someone else at another time, yet we are in bed with our partner having sex with them. In order for the addict to build communication, trust has to be acquired through our partners' seeing our willingness to halt our addictions and establish sincerity in building our relationships with them.

In the process of building a relationship with our partner, we may be involved in couples counseling or using other community resources, such as Twelve Step meetings and sponsors. As we build our communication about our needs in our relationships, we begin to build intimacy with our partner again. Intimacy is the place where we can talk about our vulnerable emotions, which allows us also to talk about our sexual needs with our partner.

When we get to the point of beginning to define our sexual needs in the relationship, which we haven't previously discussed with our partner, a great deal of conflict can come up in us. If I express my needs to my partner, for whom I have been the provider, questioning if they will acknowledge my needs is a very sensitive issue. For the one who has received those sexual needs, they may have fear of being more directly involved in sexual interaction with another person in providing for their needs. This is no longer a fantasy. It is a real time relationship in the present with our partner, in which they are not in control. For the person who has been providing for their partner's needs, to communicate what their sexual needs are could be a very vulnerable state for them. Their partner could reject their request. We have moved from a position of a conditional sexual relationship with our partner to an unconditional sexual relationship, which can fulfill both partners' needs.

In the beginning it may cause a break-down of their arousal. In time it becomes incredibly satisfying because we are in the relationship in the here and now with our partners, fulfilling their sexual needs along with our own. Our actual time of having a sexual encounter is trivial to the amount of time we engage in a relationship with our partner. Providing for our partner's sexual needs and our own, in the present moment will help to fortify our commitment to our relationship in other areas.

We also need to review our pursuit of, or prior involvement in sexual relationships with others. In some cases we may have acted out as an aggressor in the sexual relationship fulfilling our sexual appetite in objectifying our partner as a trophy. Through seduction and intercourse with them we have attained something of value. Then, we quickly lose interest in them and pursue the next relationship. In pursuing another person we take energy away from our partner that we would normally have provided to them. This is a common character defect; the grass is greener on the other side of the fence. When we put our energy into fantasy relationships with another person, it may develop into getting my needs met partially from that person, but I should be getting them met by my partner. This can also be seen in obsessive use of pornography. This is destructive when it takes away from other elements of our life. By doing so, it is undermining the relationship with our significant other. One needs to ask: Is it taking away from providing for a satisfying sexual relationship with my partner? Is fantasy causing me to distance myself from my partner? These questions must be asked through the Fourth Step to come to a full understanding of its effect on our lives. If we don't face our actions here we will not be able to plot a healthy course in our present relationship, or future relationships.

There are those individuals who have shut down their sexual needs, becoming neutral in their interaction with others. It is important for these individuals to discuss how this has impacted their ability to develop intimacy in their lives. We are all sexual beings, through our interactions with others we learn and develop sexual behavior. To deny one's sexual needs can be a form of self-destructive behavior for the recovering addict. This is an area necessary to inventory for our healing to continue.

It is also important to assess where we may have been sexually abused and violated by others, being strangers or someone we know. It is important to face this part of our inventory with an open heart. Without this effort to bring light into our emotional wounds, we will continue to leave a part of our spirit locked behind the prison. It isn't our penance to live in the dark, rather our need to nurture and heal the part of our selves that was violated. These issues are emotional scars which need to be identified and brought to the surface. It wasn't our fault for the abuse, we were victims, and we as the guardian of our spirit have a need to bring love and care to the most fragile part of our being.

This topic matter is not just for heterosexual individuals but also for homosexual individuals in developing a healthy sense of their own identity. I refrained to mention examples that occurred for the gay community, only because of my lack of expertise in the area.

There are many different types of Fourth Step inventories. To make it a thorough process we suggest you review the areas in your life where you interact in relationships, which is as follows: Identifying where I may have acted out in an offender role, where my control issues had been verbally, physically or emotionally abusive. Identifying where I was in the victim role and I was subject to verbal, physical or emotional abuse. Also identifying patterns in which I have been a victim of circumstances, in which may have occurred in my life leaving unresolved trauma. Or, through dissociation identifying if I made myself unavailable in relationships, causing damage to my relationships and myself.

Relationships with Family: In what ways have I been in a pattern of a victim, offender or isolator in my relationships with family; or what ways have I disassociated or isolated myself in my responsibilities in being part of my family?

Relationships with Friends and Acquaintances: Is my relationship with old and new friends, either close or casual, acting out a pattern of being a victim, offender or isolator?

Relationship to our Physical needs: Have I been self-destructive in taking care of my health? Have I neglected my nutritional needs and diet, my exercise, and my dental and medical needs?

Relationships based on Sexuality: Is our sense of identity in our victim, offender or isolator relationships related to our sexual behavior? This may be through our pursuit of a sexual partner and involvement in any sexual relationships, with our consent or through violation. It depends on our ability to provide for our partners needs and their willingness to provide for ours. Have we dismissed our sexual needs by not pursuing any sexual relationships due to unresolved conflicts?

Relationships based on Society: Is our sense of identity based on our victim, offender or isolation from relationships within society: on the job, in school, or involvement with probation or the criminal system? Have I intimidated people, or been the victim of intimidation? Do I have prejudices or single out individuals due to their race, color of their skin, age, sexual preference, weight, religious beliefs or gender? Have I been open to learning about my own cultural traditions that were part of my heritage?

Relationships in Public: Is our sense of identity based on our victim, offender or isolation from interactions with others in public areas, such as restaurants, bars, grocery stores, movie theaters or on the road, through road rage or reckless driving, etc.?

Relationships based on Spirituality: Is our sense of identity in context to our spiritual beliefs and practices? Have we accused others of being morally wrong because their religious beliefs are not the same as our own? Are we in a victim pattern because of our religious upbringing, feeling guilty about our actions and judging ourselves accordingly; or relying on a spiritual guide for approval for any good feelings we have about ourselves? Have I withdrawn from those religious/spiritual ties out of avoidance of unresolved conflict?

Creating an attitude of willingness isn't enough. It is through hard-felt emotion that we have taken on the effort to work on the prior Steps leading up to this autobiography and moral inventory. Having an emotional awareness that my past is a roadmap of my life experience, and facing this with pen to paper is at hand. I can't say that it is the only way to recovery, but an old relapse polka I heard put it like this:, "One, two, three, slip; one, two, three, slip." (Slip is a term in recovery referring to a relapse.) Procrastination hinders a lot of our commitment to do this Step.

I once was sponsoring a doctor in recovery and I was on him for about four months to do his inventory. I finally told him I wanted him to write a Fourth Step on his patterns of procrastination in his life. He then followed through, which started the process of looking into his past.

I have often seen people who never completed their Fourth Step, lack the motivation to follow through with the remaining Steps. Most of us fear what lies in our past, yet we have been living with this content inside of us our entire lives. It's true that most people perceive the Fourth Step as a huge catapult in recovery, but still, we fear that facing ourselves will be a horrid experience.

I knew a person who felt this way finally just sit down and do the Fourth Step. After finishing, he reported the person he discovered inside was a beautiful child of God who deserved a second chance.

This Fourth Step is a powerful tool which looks through the window of our past with tools that assist us in viewing the experience, as it was, without judgment. Our attitude going into writing out a Fourth Step is important to acknowledge as we start this process.

The first time I did a Fourth Step, I was writing it out with reservations because of my fear-based reaction to compliance. I was in legal trouble and needed to complete what was required from me at the inpatient facility I was in. I thought that if I sounded good enough I would pass the requirements for treatment, but my sincerity wasn't there. Even though the content of what I was writing probably would have been adequate for most people, it wasn't really me who I was writing about. So it is important to recognize who I am doing this for and be able to identify what internal motivators I have to continue with my recovery, before doing the list.

Having a private, safe place to write out your Fourth Step is important. This is a private thing, so be sure to give yourself a place of solitude where you can do it. You need that safe haven so you can concentrate on the task at hand.

There are many methods we can use to write out this Fourth Step (autobiographical history) of our actions. There are Fourth Step guides available on the internet. You may also find Fourth Step guides pertaining to specific addictions through Narcotics Anonymous, Hazelden Publications, and Celebrate Recovery, to name a few. Or hop to our web site at: www.12StepsUnlocked.com for a Fourth Step guide.

I have suggested for recovering addicts to set up an appointment a week or two from when they start writing, to present it to their sponsor, clergy or counselor. This time limit usually sets the process in motion. You must be prepared before you start such an important task. If you are in a crisis of some sort, financial or emotional, it is not the time to begin a Fourth Step. Be calm. Have a binder (or journal) so you can keep everything together. Work chronologically. It is difficult to take on a task that you know will probably trigger negative feelings about yourself, so it common to experience some anxiety or mild depression in writing out your life experience. Don't feel like you are the only one who is experiencing this reaction. Keep in mind that it is important not only to write about our negative experiences, but also our positive ones; not just our character defects, but our character assets as well.

People in recovery tend to focus on one aspect of their personality, this is a full inventory. It is tough to look at positives when you have only been looking at all the negatives. In a moral inventory, we tend to judge ourselves sharply, but that sharp criticism isn't what we are after in this Fourth Step. What we need now is an objective view of ourselves at this stage of awareness in our lives. Making sponsors, mentors, and/or others in recovery aware that you are working on your Fourth Step solidifies your commitment to doing it. It also gives you a back-up support system if you need to talk about some of the feelings which are being triggered. It is important to keep the material you are writing in a private and secure place.

I once had a client in an inpatient facility work on his Fourth Step in his room. His wife came to visit him and read the work on his nightstand. This spurred a lot of problems in their relationship.

The purpose of this initial autobiography is to write about our lives as we see it today. There will be other opportunities to write on the subject in the future when we may have gained more insight into ourselves. Right now, give yourself time. You don't have to write it out all at once. A week or two is a good time frame. That is enough time for you to write a thorough account. Remember, after beginning a Fourth Step other issues could arise. This process of writing isn't something we do every day. It is there for the occasions when we feel the need to review our lives. It may be necessary to repeat it after a relapse, a divorce, or some other life-changing event. I have written a Fourth Step about every seven years in my recovery over the past 35 years. A person is ready to write out a Fourth Step when a past event or experience is preventing him or her from living in the here and now. In doing so, there is a tremendous benefit.

Once I heard that a Persian rug is woven with only one thread throughout the entire weave. The thread of our life experience is our timeline. Through writing our life experience, we weave our story with our motives and intent alongside our actions. We see how often fear was the basis for certain character defects and that a lot of choices we made in our lives were fear-based. This personal realization gives us the fortitude to break free from some of these patterns in our lives.

Writing out a Fourth Step is like fasting for a period of time. I may be uncomfortable in the process, but it is releasing toxins from my body. Often I have heard about people having unpleasant feelings and having almost flu like symptoms when writing it out. This is why it is important to have a sponsor or accountability partner available for support. Feeling badly doesn't mean that this is a bad experience, but one that reflects a lot of emotions which we have held inside and are becoming aware. I remember a similar situation in a training I received on Interferon which was prescribed for Hepatitis C carriers. They reported flu like symptoms that left them feeling poorly. It was explained that the flu like symptoms was the person's own immune system kicking in, fighting the disease back.

Don't forget to read through the Fourth Step often. Re-readings may trigger other memories that you have been withholding. Keep a copy of your Fourth Step handy for assistance in working on Step Six and Step Eight.

Remember this: Only when I feel in my gut that this Step is an open portrayal of who I have been, is it time to move on to the next Step.

Step Five

Admitted to God, to ourselves, and to another human being the exact nature of our wrongs.

So we have completed our Fourth Step and have it in hand ready to present to our sponsor, counselor, clergy or other. To verbally present it takes a lot of effort. We have just written an honest and thorough inventory of our life's actions and we may be prone to hesitate.

The shame and isolation of our addictions told us that we were different from others in our core beliefs about ourselves. In the Fourth Step we take action by sharing this with another person and God as we understand Him. This reference positions us to share a very personal element of who we are with the outside world.

We usually took parts of our past experience and shared it with people who are prone to co-sign our previous addictive behaviors, which kept us from making personal change. This is an effort to share the most sensitive and vulnerable information about ourselves with one person. We are at the edge of a cliff, not being able to see what the outcome will be. This is firming up our position in taking the concepts of recovery and putting them into action. In proceeding with this Step we are continuing the effort from the previous Steps in trusting something outside of ourselves.

This is a deeper conviction of trust that we are taking, we haven't been let down up to now. When we let our presence be known in the Twelve Step meetings by saying "my name is _____, and I am an addict or alcoholic," we were heard and welcomed. When we sat down and reviewed our First Step with our sponsor, counselor or Twelve Step group we felt the outside shell of our hardened denial peeling away. In Step Two, when we came to believe that there was a Power greater than ourselves, we felt hope for the first time in a long time. We were able to ask for help and became teachable. In the Third Step we were willing to let go of control and trust a force outside of ourselves. This Step of action provides us with the strength to make change in our lives by taking direction and implementing it into our lives. The bi-product of this gives us the feeling of being part of something greater than ourselves. The Fourth Step took us to a new awareness of ourselves and this effort took tremendous courage. We found a new realization of ourselves bringing light to the dark corners of our past. This effort up to now has proven remarkable, we are not alone anymore. We know that the footsteps we have taken are unfolding a path where we see encouragement in the person we are becoming.

Most of us are concerned of what others will think of us if we share our true feelings, thoughts and actions. This Fifth Step is taken by sharing our experiences with one person, and a loving God of our understanding. This effort is building the strength in belief not only of a loving God, but of trusting another human being. This effort fortifies our trust in our relationship with another. This roadmap to recovery leaves us with the risk of trusting others with our secrets which we have been holding onto throughout our lives. This effort breaks through the final grains of denial which have been lingering in our thoughts about our past addictions. It brings us, again to the forefront of our minds, a clearer picture of our past. Here is where we need to focus on the safest and most direct route on this path of recovery. This roadmap will define clarity of purpose.

Granted, this effort of sharing your Fifth Step with another person is like jumping into the deep end of a swimming pool, but often what we find there is a way to build trust with others who are accepting of us. In this Fifth Step, we may share a large part of who we are in many relationships. Our listener and our Higher Power are going to hear the entire picture of our life experiences, the good with the bad.

When we set up an appointment to present our Fifth Step, we are showing the person we selected to hear it that we are serious about our recovery. Who we select is a personal decision. Some people, in their first attempt at presenting a Fifth Step, may feel more comfortable sharing with someone from the clergy or a counselor who also is in recovery. This type of listener is bound by professional confidentiality to keep your information private. There are, of course, certain exceptions, such as when the person doing the Fifth Step reports to the listener that they intend to cause or have caused physical or sexual harm to someone. But for most of us, the report is going to remain confidential, which provides a sense of security, especially for those presenting for the first time.

I always suggest that the person chosen to hear the Fifth Step should also be in Twelve Step recovery. This way, the presenter knows that the person listening understands the process of this Step. Using a sponsor is the time-honored method of processing a Fifth Step. Even if you do process the Fifth Step with a professional, I suggest you also share it with your sponsor. That person should know you and your needs by now, so trust him or her in this process. Having a quiet place to share this Step is suggested. It is important to provide a safe place while we bring these experiences and emotions to the surface.

We are not simply sharing our Fourth Step by processing our Fifth Step. We are acknowledging and accepting the exact nature of our wrongs. This means we must take into consideration our intent in sharing the information at hand. Am I looking for some type of further gain besides sharing it with another person?

The first time I shared a Fifth Step, I was in legal trouble. I was in a treatment center, trying to remain in compliance to avoid the legal issues I was facing. I thought if I completed the Fifth Step, I would be doing what others expected of me. Then, once I met their expectations, I believed I could go back to being in control of my life again.

Moving from compliance to acceptance of a problem, I internalized the reasons for change occurring in my life. As I said before, most people face their issues as a result of some type of intervention. There are external consequences that drive them to addressing their problem in the beginning. Eventually, however, a person has to move from external motivators for change to internal motivators for change. As said before, we must be able to identify reasons for ourselves to proceed with trusting something or someone outside of ourselves. This is a difficult adjustment because our condition of not trusting others is a core issue underlying addictions. We are transforming our beliefs into a new perspective. How can we be sure we are ready for this Step? By not being invested in what the outcome of this Step will provide. Again, it takes trusting something outside of us which we don't understand. We become invested in sharing this sensitive material in the Fifth Step, but not to enhance a position of control back into our lives. It becomes evident to us that this is a natural transition in becoming more than what we thought we were. We are doing this Step because it will reassure us in taking further steps away from the emptiness of addiction.

To begin the Fifth Step, you may say a simple prayer with your sponsor, asking your Higher Power, or loving God of your understanding to be present during this time. Sharing a prayer with our sponsor or person who is there can offer strength to present this fearless, moral inventory.

I had a client set up an appointment to share his Fifth Step. He was wilderness oriented, so I took him on a hike. At the top of a tall ridge we built a fire. To get things started I began with a prayer and asked the client to pray too, because the Step requires the sharing be done with God as well as another person. I usually ask God, as we understand Him, to place a circle of protection around us while we are processing this Step. As the man began to share, snow began to fall. His sharing took almost two hours and when he was done we looked around and saw about 3 inches of snowfall on the ground. We noticed it was dry in a fifteen foot perfect circle around us. Yes, science may prove that it was the heat rising from the fire that caused the circle of snow to be melted, but it still was an experience of significance to both of us.

It is important to keep an open mind to the presence of a loving force in our lives being with us during our Fifth Step, even if we are Atheist or Agnostic. Believing there is a loving God or Power outside of us involved in our success in recovery strengthens our efforts. Once we begin to share, we may feel nervous and our gut may feel like jelly. We may have a quiver in our voice as we go over our inventory. When we look up, however, we see care and reassurance from our sponsor, counselor or person we asked to listen to our Fifth Step. The person listening may ask questions pertaining to what we are sharing. They may inject personal experience similar to what we are sharing. We may even laugh at the absurdity of some of the lies we told to cover our tracks of our addictions. When we share openly with another person about our experiences and engage in interaction, we can begin to see that our experiences were common to others; and the severity of judgment we made about ourselves wasn't warranted. Although the person we chose is there for us in the same time honored way many others have been there for others in sharing their Fifth Step, they may need to know other details and will ask questions.

Presenting the exact nature of our wrongs to another person, we are sharing not only the lies we told to others and ourselves, but the underlying motive that fed our addictions. Here are some examples: The addict who continued their personal selfishness and self-serving behaviors caused others to suffer; The person who continued to be abused from one relationship to another failed to look at the lack of self-care and nurturing that had placed them in harm's way; The victim of circumstance continued to abuse their substances to numb their pain, creating an unresolved sense of grief and trauma; The person who avoided any intimacy with others created a prison of isolation in their addictions. All of these are the underlying thread that put us in patterns of being isolators, offenders and victims to others and ourselves. If I don't see the core issues under these violations I cannot learn another course of action. The Fifth Step paints a picture that weaves throughout our lives. How can we escape the maze if we don't realize it was the construction of our own doing? I want to assure you that I am not placing responsibility onto the victim who was raped while intoxicated, placing them in harm's way. I am putting responsibility on the addiction that robbed the person of the clarity of mind and safety, which placed them within reach of their offenders. The offender was the one who was responsible for the abuse they perpetrated. However, predators will seek out prey that is accessible and vulnerable.

There is a tremendous release of guilt, shame, pain and fear when we are sharing our Fifth Step. There may be a lot of things that we share during this time to which we keep a restrained emotional response. We are awakening emotions that have remained deep within ourselves. As said before, there are no guarantees of the outcome. This can bring other issues to the surface that will need to be continued at a later date for closure. It is a doorway that we are opening for the purpose of not only building the ability to share our emotions with others, but to gain insight and acceptance of the wreckage of our past.

We may wait to share the most sensitive materials of our past at the end of our Fifth Step. As long as we present this information about our victimization, patterns of abuse of others, or intense isolation from others, we have done our job. Often it is hard for us to list the positive aspects of our life experience when we have delved into the depth of our darkest memories. We may not feel the words as being positive, but it is important to share our strengths.

Make sure that you have a lot of water with you during your presentation. Why? Because when we are stressed we become dehydrated and it is important to feel clear headed during our presentation. We are astounded by the interest our sponsor or support person, in hearing our presentation, offered during our Fifth Step. Often there is a feeling of deep relief when we look up at their eyes and see acceptance from them. Often we feel like we just swam the English Channel in completing this effort. Many of us had been plagued by uncompleted efforts in our lives due to our addictions and fear. This valiant effort becomes complete without causing any serious harm to ourselves. In fact, it just brought us intensely closer to another human being.

It gets confusing for most of us thinking that this Step aids us in a spiritual awakening when in fact most of us don't even know what that really means. To begin with, we are creating an emotional awakening of an internal voice that had been silenced for a long time. We see hope beginning to build in our efforts towards a life in recovery. Not only are we leaving behind a lifestyle of addiction, but we are growing into a person with dignity and maturity. This concept of an awakening of our spiritual nature means that we are not alone in this world.

We may hear from others what their experience was in sharing their Fifth Step at a meeting. We see that it was a positive experience for everyone who worked the Step and brought further meaning to their lives. After sharing this with another person, often we feel a sense of relief. We have taken a giant leap of faith by revealing the entire image of who we are to another person. We have looked deeply into their eyes, searching for acceptance. If we have found it, we feel a sense of deliverance from the isolation that we have been living with. Not only are we beginning to trust in relationships, but we are bringing a true sense of awareness into our own lives. We have shared our most inward secrets and were not rejected. 'The cat's out of the bag', and our ability to share with others becomes easier.

Yes, there is a lot more work to be done, but we now have hope. We see that our past does not define us, that we will not always remain stuck. By sharing our load with another person we free ourselves of the confines of our perpetual prison. If I have had a limp for years, and I simply rest the muscles by not walking for a period of time, I will continue, in the long run, to have the limp. If however, I do rehabilitative work to build strength in both of my legs and use other resources to assist my balance, I might be able to return to a normal pattern of walking.

Many people go through their entire lives without feeling a sense of purpose, driven to alter their direction. Working the Fifth Step helps remove the obstacles in our lives which makes our path in recovery less tedious.

I was in a halfway house in Minneapolis called Progress Valley when an artist who had gone through the program donated a painting he made in gratitude to them. It was a man on a path leading down into a beautiful valley. Fourteen years later, I was visiting a treatment program in Phoenix called Valley of Hope. On the wall I noticed a picture by the same artist. It was the same landscape but now he was further down the path.

In our Fifth Step it is important to share everything that we are aware of with our listener in recovery.

When I was in treatment for the second, and last time in a program called Pharm House, in Minneapolis, an old minister came in to listen to the Fifth Steps. My effort was thorough and he was attentive to everything I said. Although I was very precise in sharing specific actions of mine, at the end he asked, "Is there anything else that was significant that you would like to share?" I told him about two incidents which were not criminal, but I felt extremely bad about because they had so negatively affected my family. At the end, he looked into my eyes and said "good job."

After processing a Fifth Step, it is helpful to save the Fourth Step document. This can come in valuable for processing Step Six and Step Eight. By sharing this information, it is now part of our awareness in our lives. We can continue to move on from building trust with our listener to building relationships with people who serve as part of our recovery. We now can alter how we perceive the past and its chains of shame, guilt, pain and fear. We have faced ourselves in the mirror and stated that our future does not have to be bound by that behavior. We have gone beyond the awareness in our lives of going through crisis to crisis. We now see how our character defects weaved throughout our lives. This sets the stage for Step Six.

Step Six

Were entirely ready to have God remove all these defects of character.

Again we have to create an attitude of preparation in Step Six, before taking action in Step Seven.

The Steps are set up as a process to follow, not to be done in a random manner. If we jumped Steps Six and Seven and made amends, we haven't yet disengaged the weapon that creates further destruction in our lives. We have to disarm ourselves from the character defects that continue to cause havoc and chaos in our lives.

We may have some reservations here because, again, control is something we struggle in giving up. If I let go of all my character defects, what will I have left? I stood silently in fear the first time I heard this Step. I thought of an image of me being mindless, giving away recovery literature on a street corner. At first I thought if I gave up all my character defects there wouldn't be anything left. I don't think that any of us has the ability to get rid of all of our character defects, let's face it: some of them are just too much fun. No one is going to turn us into someone we don't want to be. Yes, we have the ability to change our relationships with others, but that is always our choice.

In the first few years of looking at this Step I was plagued by my old religious upbringing, waiting for some type of miraculous event to occur that would change my life. I was waiting for the burning bush to occur in my life and it never happened. God isn't going to reach down and pluck out our character defects, it would be nice if was that simple, but it isn't. Part of my awakening is letting go of my view that the world is changing, because the rules that I set for my actions in relation to others are changing. My ability to see the world clearly had begun by changing my playgrounds and playmates. In recovery, through our interactions with peers at Twelve Step meetings, we build a network of true friends. Real friends tell us what we want to hear; true friends tell us unbridled perspective which helps shape our recovery. This network of support offers us insight into our actions, by hanging around smarter people we get smarter. This new insight brings out the flaws that have been coming to the surface as a result of working the Steps and in my activity in Twelve Step meetings. Again the old adage that if one person tells you that you have a tail don't worry about it, but if two or three state it, you had better turn around and see if it is wagging.

Our emotions have also awoken, so when we act out on one of our less endearing traits we are struck with shame, guilt and remorse for our actions. We feel sick to our stomachs sometimes and mumble out the words, "I'm sorry." We feel regret but we don't know how to make effective change in our actions and lives to correct the course. We may get frustrated that our character defects are causing harm in our new relationships in recovery. We may try to suppress our character defects, and it comes out more like a large sandwich being squeezed together. The contents of our behavior, like the sandwich, starts to ooze out in a sideways manner. We may try to hold back our behavior but we find ourselves stumbling over and over again on some of these negative traits.

We are on a course for clearing the obstructions that are cluttering our path in recovery. We see the need to remove these defects of character. We see these behaviors as unflattering and try to immediately discard them, but like an annoying hiccup they keep coming back. By being in recovery and changing these behaviors we find there is a course of action to be followed, which we will discuss in this Step.

We need to remember the tools we learned earlier in the Steps: Step One: I can't; Step Two: We can; and Step Three: Let's do it! These principles give us the tools necessary to truly negotiate the changes required for the rest of the Steps to work. Yes, we start off with basic skills and put them into action and as we work through each Step we build more awareness and confidence. Think of each Step moving deeper and deeper into our lives so that they are fully integrated into a healthy, positive lifestyle of recovery.

The Fifth Step gave us the awareness of problems in our lives. I become more aware of a behavior once I acknowledge its presence. Due to our awakened state of awareness and emotions, our perception starts to surface. Similar to when any of us have went out and bought a car, how often over the next few months do we notice that same car being driven on the road? The car had been around just as much, but we weren't aware of it because the more trivial information that isn't as important in our everyday life is stored in a less conscious state of awareness. Similarly we become aware of a character defect occurring in our lives, we see how often we are doing that character defect and how often other people are also. This piece of information is being stored in a part of our brain placing it in our conscious awareness.

By now we have an awareness of our character defects and we are entirely ready to have God remove them. Along with awareness comes social responsibility for our actions. We know that these character defects, which we use as protective mechanisms when we are in some type of crisis, have led to our separation in relationships. I often have done character defect assignments in treatment with clients. In the assignment I ask, "What is the primary character defect you wish to change?" Then I ask them, "What has this character defect given to you?" and "What has this character defect taken from you?" They usually give some self-serving or self-protecting reason for having the character defect. When I ask what it took from them, the answer is pretty much the same that I hear from recovering people: The character defect leaves them isolated and alone and empty spiritually.

I use the example of being a scapegoat when I was in relationships and I was playing the bad boy in my addiction. This gave me empowerment over others because I intimidated them. But being the antagonist created distance and isolation in my relationships with others. When I worked through that character defect, it brought me intimacy in my relationships.

Most inpatient treatment centers will urge the client to initially work through their primary character defect. This is the one that is interfering with us working on recovery. (Often through our recovery, we will find victim, offender and isolating behaviors that need to be addressed to improve our recovery.) Character defects are a defense mechanism, which add to our denial of addiction. They are an integral part of layers of imprisonment that have alienated us from our relationships. By becoming aware of what the behaviors have taken from us, we set the stage for creating an attitude and motivation for change.

Awareness is the first step to this new design for living. What the character defect has cost us is always the same: it left us alone and isolated. We tackle one character defect at a time because the amount of work needed for each is overwhelming. The phrase "easy does it" comes to mind. I remember at meetings early in my recovery hearing the term, "Scratch it when it itches and don't worry about the whole pile, just deal with what's on the top." This attitude makes it tolerable for us to make change on a gradual basis. We're not looking for perfection, just progress in our recovery.

As we spoke about earlier, character defects can be broken down into three patterns as we try to cope with problems in our lives: we fight, we freeze or we flee. These character defect styles can be described as offender, victim, or isolating patterns. It would benefit us to review the characteristics of these behaviors so we can see them more clearly.

Offender patterns struggle to become the dominant role in a relationship. The person in the offender role develops rigid expectations of others while having little or no expectations of themselves, which allows them to be judge and jury to others in the relationship. They struggle with control of people, places and things in an attempt to feel a sense of control. This role is their price tag to be in a relationship. One does not play the offender in all relationships, only those that fulfill their personal needs. The offender role usually surfaces with family members, maybe with people at work or with personal friendships, in our church or in other areas where we interact with others.

In character defects I have to be aware that if my behavior offends someone that I am in a relationship with, then I am responsible to change that behavior. I need to do this if I wish to remain in a resentment free relationship. We give up the power that being in control offered us for the simplicity of unconditional relationships. Our relationships become spontaneous with an amazing lack of stress, because we don't need to be in control.

The victim role is another primary role of interaction. It is easy to identify. Victims have rigid expectations for themselves but not for others they are in a primary relationship with. They are frozen in a relationship with an offender or dominant personality type. The price they pay to be in that relationship is their burden to claim responsibility. They think everything, in some way, is their fault; or they are blamed for circumstances and are compliant in accepting responsibility. By allowing choices to be made for them, they are avoiding conflict and responsibility for making other decisions on their own.

Being aware of my victim roles that I am still doing is necessary for taking this Step. It is easy to spot my victim roles, because I am usually feeling useless, hopeless and less than others in those relationships. That doesn't mean I am, but I must do something to correct the course for recovery to occur. These victim patterns will trigger depression and low self-esteem in a person which can block a person's progress from finding a solution. Acknowledging a violation of your personal boundaries, being abused or victimized, will often trigger embarrassment or shame. These feelings cause a person to shut down. It might help to take smaller steps, by talking with a sponsor or counselor about the circumstances. Yes, if we move into a pattern of victimization, as a guardian of our recovery it is necessary to reach out for help from others.

I have seen people in recovery flip from being an offender in their family, friends and social interactions, to becoming a victim. Due to guilt and shame about their actions, they switched to moralizing about their behavior, making themselves out to be bad people. Another example is where family members weren't able to let go of their long term resentments towards the alcoholic or addict in their life. The addicted person had stopped using and came into recovery. However, family members continued to believe they were still using or dishonest, placing them in a scapegoat role. When this occurs, it is important for the person to have patience with family, because we have done them harm in the past. They have reasons to be suspicious. With assistance of a sponsor, counselor or other friends in recovery we have the tools to bring our lives in perspective. I am responsible for what my actions are in my relationships today. The others we may have harmed may take time to heal.

Isolating character defects are a way of keeping our actions hidden from others. We develop methods of avoiding conflict, but it also causes us to avoid intimacy in our relationships. This person uses fantasy, physically withdrawing from others, or uses other manners of escapism. Some examples are through playing video games, watching television or movies, reading, using the internet or other time consuming activities. Of course we all use these as casual forms of entertainment, but these individuals use them as a primary preoccupation to escape relationships.

Procrastination is a simple concept of avoidance that is self-indulging by not doing anything. These behaviors are one of the biggest traps that trigger relapse. For example, we stop going to meetings or calling our sponsor. We find excuses to avoid intimate conversations by changing the subject or using humor to switch the focus. Another form of this escapism is working all the time. We call these people workaholics, and the gratification that one gets is the monetary benefit and control. These people know how to function on a job, but are full of the feeling of inadequacy in dealing with everyday life. They feel more in control on the job than in their real life. I'm not telling you to quit your job, but a person needs to have balance in their relationships with the people who bring meaning in their life. Using dissociation, the addict flees from relationships with others through fantasy or sometimes even physically distancing themselves in relationships. In a defensive mode of self-protection, they simply detach from interpersonal relationships.

For instance, a client named Larry said he had been quiet but angry inside since childhood. It turned out he had a long pattern of a dominant foster parent controlling him. Larry married an addict who was outwardly abusive towards him, but he was able to manage the household. Larry was functional at his job maintaining an income and paying the bills. He used pot and alcohol in a binging fashion as an outlet for stress. Larry was prone to character defects of isolation, in which he worked through with continued individual counseling after he got through treatment. He worked on these issues and has been sober for over the past three years attending his outside Twelve Step meetings. Breaking free from his character defects has gotten him out of procrastination in his primary life choices and into being assertive and proactive in his recovery.

In working this Step most of us will be able to become aware of offender, victim and isolating character defects in our lives. Our job here is to acknowledge them and to recognize the impact it has had, not only on our lives but others around us. This awareness comes about by using the resources to our disposal in the relationships we have built as part of our recovery. We ask for feedback and support in changing our character defects from our sponsors, mentors in recovery and our Twelve Step meetings. Their feedback acts as mirrors to our most hidden behaviors. The strength we derive from others and our Higher Power brings us clarity of mind.

We demonstrate the courage to admit to our mistakes. By admitting our character defects we demonstrate the ability to change. Making amends isn't necessarily saying we won't do it again. It is acknowledging the impact our actions has had on someone else and our willingness to apologize for our behavior. This in itself is a step towards recovery - it reinforces our new found values.

We write down our character defects that continue to affect our lives and review them with our sponsor, counselor, or others in

Twelve Step recovery. We used our Fourth Step as a reviewing tool to recognize the patterns that had occurred in our past character defects. Also the Fourth Step is an excellent resource to reflect on the patterns of our character defects and how they had been anchored in our life. With this information we can see more clearly how they are played out in our present day lives. Your Fourth Step can be handy as a tool not only in this Sixth Step, but also in the Eighth Step. Again this is a format that can be used to review our character defects in our lives today.

Relationships with family: In what ways have I been in a pattern of a victim, offender or isolator in my relationships with family; or what ways have I disassociated or isolated myself in my responsibilities in being part of my family?

Relationships with friends and acquaintances: Is my relationship with old and new friends, either close or casual, acting out a pattern of being a victim, offender or isolator?

Relationship to our physical needs: Have I been self-destructive in taking care of my health? Have I neglected my nutritional needs and diet, my exercise, and my dental and medical needs?

Relationships based on Sexuality: Is our sense of identity in our victim, offender or isolator relationships related to our sexual behavior? This may be through our pursuit of a sexual partner and involvement in any sexual relationships, with our consent or through violation. It depends on our ability to provide for our partners needs and their willingness to provide for ours. Have we dismissed our sexual needs by not pursuing any sexual relationships due to unresolved conflicts?

Relationships based on Society: Is our sense of identity based on our victim, offender or isolation from relationships within society: on the job, in school, or involvement with probation or the criminal system? Have I intimidated people, or been the victim of intimidation? Do I have prejudices or single out individuals due to their race, color of their skin, age, sexual preference, weight, religious beliefs or gender? Have I been open to learning about my own cultural traditions that were part of my heritage?

Relationships in Public: Is our sense of identity based on our victim, offender or isolation from interactions with others in public areas, such as restaurants, bars, grocery stores, movie theaters or on the road, through road rage or reckless driving, etc.?

Relationships based on Spirituality: Is our sense of identity in context to our spiritual beliefs and practices? Have we accused others of being morally wrong because their religious beliefs are not the same as our own? Are we in a victim pattern because of our religious upbringing, feeling guilty about our actions and judging ourselves accordingly; or relying on a spiritual guide for approval for any good feelings we have about ourselves? Have I withdrawn from those religious/spiritual ties out of avoidance of unresolved conflict?

We get feedback from others as they serve to be mirrors for us reflecting our actions. We have found understanding and patience from others in recovery. The effort we have taken in interacting with others about this Step has brought encouragement and hope. Our sponsor and others in the program emanate the character assets we are working to achieve. We see hope through the success of recovery, which we see in the eyes and life of those at the meetings. We have made a thorough effort to become aware of our character defects and are prepared to move onto Step Seven.

Step Seven

Humbly asked Him to remove our shortcomings.

The term "humbly" is placed at the beginning of the Step. Again, humility develops as we are capable of building relationships with others. In Step Two we asked for help, and in Step Three we began to embrace our relationships with the outside world being willing to receive the help from others. The term humility which I read in the Webster Dictionary made a lot of sense to me. It stated 'a realistic appraisal of our limitations and assets in connection with others.' This gives us an understanding that our fallibility and our strengths as human beings are equal to all. Each of us has a vision of the world that is unique to us and we have the ability to express that vision to others. The first word in the First Step is "We" and is set there because it is the source for our success in recovery from addictions. We build our relationships with others in association through the same personal commitment to change, and the desire to halt our addictions. All the work that we do in working the Steps is there to remove the obstacles which stop us from embracing our relationships with others.

Step Six prepared us for an attitude of awareness and being teachable in our lives. Step Seven then unfolds into the next action Step. The Seventh Step points directly to our concept of God and says 'humbly asked God to remove these shortcomings.' We are in a place of motivation toward change in our lives through all the work that we have done up to now. Our image that we have gotten so familiar with in addiction has pretty much been the same; in control or out of control we remained the same. In recovery we see that our lives and relationships are changing. Who we are changing into is the unknown and we rely upon guidance from our Higher Power.

The Seventh Step Prayer, *"My Creator, I am now willing that You should have all of me, good and bad. I pray that You now remove from me every single defect of character which stands in the way of my usefulness to You and my fellows. Grant me strength as I go from here to do Your bidding. Amen."* (Big Book of *Alcoholic's Anonymous, Into Action, page 76*.) This prayer is said in many other ways, for self-protection and guidance along a path that we have no control over. The need to be vulnerable, to not knowing the outcome, is necessary so that we may be flexible in allowing the design of our recovery to take a new direction. We are not pre-programming results. We are being open to what possibilities may come into our lives.

We can no longer point the finger at others and use blame or resentment to cover up our tracks. We realize it is our doing that brought about our own problems. So letting go of control of our relationships with others is the journey laid out before us. In letting go of our past need to be in control and giving it over to a Power greater than ourselves, we allow this force, a loving God of our understanding, to shape us into the person we are becoming.

To live in the solution, I have to be willing to use the positive characteristics of my assets to build a new life. I replace my character defects with the positive values that each one of us have. I begin to live with unconditional relationships based on a mutual realization that I am no greater and no less than any other individual. To live by the principle "do unto others as you would have them do unto you" is our goal in recovery. These are spiritual and moral aspirations; they are a direction that we are working toward.

We can't work them perfectly, but by applying these principles to our lives we improve the quality of our recovery. We have taken great strides to see how our actions have affected our lives. We have recognized that our character defects clearly have impacted our ability to develop intimacy in relationships. But now we go back to that initial fear of vulnerability. We wonder: if we remove the behavior, who will we be? There is a sense of entitlement associated with this behavior that goes deep in our roots. It has become a sense of identity for us. So who are we becoming now? Rooting out our engrained character defects leave us feeling vulnerable and without a barrier between us and our more intimate relationships. We are seeing, for the first time or for a long time, ourselves in unconditional relationships. Step Six was the preparation for the action to be taken in Step Seven.

To deal with a character defect we move from a disassociated state of awareness of the problem, which could be known as the subconscious. This effectively kept us unaware of our behavior because we were doing it on an automatic basis. Have you ever been driving your car to go somewhere, and you automatically turn heading toward your work or a location you often travel? Like a rut in my life, I can see myself going that direction. I can see my behavior and how often I am doing it, and how often other people are doing that same character defect. At first I am discouraged by the effects it is causing in my life and try to get rid of the behavior, but it comes back like a yoyo in my life's actions. It again has become a habit in my life.

The truth is it takes time for us to get to a point of deciding to change our behavior. I have seen myself become frustrated about repeating the same actions over and over again in my personal relationships. This inventory process causes a lot of stress as we start to change. We find we're not doing it perfectly and become overly judgmental of ourselves. Having a new peer group that encourages healthy personal change is part of the necessary reality to change these behaviors. My old friends told me what I wanted to hear and cosigned my behavior. It takes a handful of real friends in recovery to help a person make a major character defect change, or stop an addiction. I often find a lot of these friends in Twelve Step meetings.

Doing an inventory of our character defects which we did in Step Six, along with the mirror reflection of honest feedback we receive from friends in recovery brings us to another moment of clarity in our lives. Once I am on the path to personal change, I get to the point that I call a "super-conscious state of awareness." This means I am in the moment right before I react with a character defect which I am trying to change. I either take another action which is based from my character assets or I don't take that action at all. This is a personal choice we have, in living in the here and now. In those moments when we are deciding not to allow our character defect to take over, we are adding to our continued experience in helping ourselves create a different direction in our lives.

The first few steps in changing our behavior are uncomfortable and we may feel awkward about it. When we see the opportunity for the character defect to come to the forefront of our mind, instead of acting in the old behavior, we stop and simply do not engage in it. The interaction that prompted our desire to do the behavior continues; but we restrain the behavior because we know we are only using it as a defense to establish a sense of control, and to block the possibility of being hurt. We can change the interaction without the character defect.

The bi-product of not engaging in the behavior, or defect, is that we begin to build intimacy and trust in our relationships. We become part of the process rather than the instrument of the relationship. These moments turn into days and these days turn into weeks and so on. As I break free from a character defect the 'new me' emerges, based upon my strengthening character assets. We go through a grieving process in letting go of a character defect the same as the loss of any relationship. This adjustment in our perception of self will take time before we may start to feel comfortable with ourselves.

The concept of unconditional relationships brings forth a bi-product, self-esteem which stays with us. Self-esteem grows as a direct result of my actions, based on how I conduct myself in relationships. This process is a flexible set of guidelines that we use to monitor ourselves and others in our personal relationships. These actions begin with rules we set such as:

1. Setting expectations of how I should be acting in my relationships with others through the way I conduct myself. For example,

in a conversation that I am having with someone, they remark that a comment or gesture I made was offensive to them and take one step back from me. I look at my behavior and apologize to them which are met with approval and they take one step closer.

2. Setting personal expectations of how I want other people to act in their relationship towards me, defining boundaries, in accordance. For example, if someone is disrespectful towards me I will express that their actions were inappropriate and possibly end the conversation and leave.

3. My values in relationships with others and how they coincide with my spiritual belief system. Am I allowing my spiritual beliefs to be in a flexible state of change, which allows me to expand my personal growth in remaining teachable with those around me? For example, a friend asks me to attend their church service with them. Although I may find conflict with some of their practices I maintain an open mind, walking away with something of value for myself.

We can see in detail how our offender and victim character defects become resolved through a simple assessment tool in Diagram B.

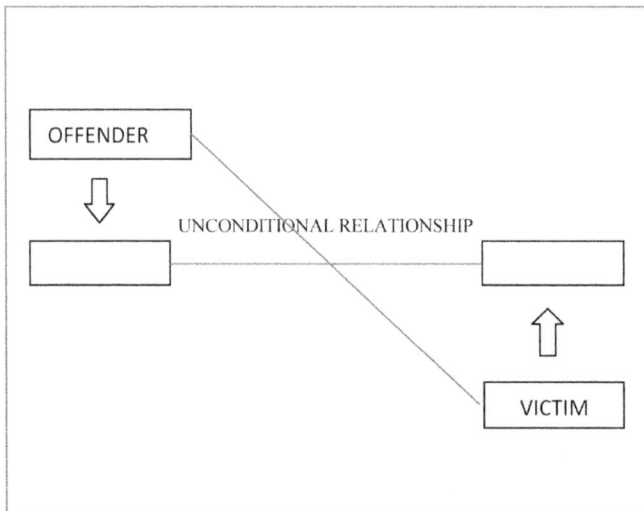

Diagram B

When we are in an offender character defect we are having rigid expectations/rules for those we are victimizing as a result of our behavior. We have no expectations/rules of our actions, thus we feel justified in controlling them. First of all we must halt the controlling behavior. Next for resolving these character defects we build a realistic set of expectations for our actions, which bring our perception of who we are to a more equal level.

The offender needs to be open to accountability for their actions by being open to listening to those they have offended. In gaining input from those we have offended, we lessen the expectations we have of them. When both offender and victim's needs are being communicated in an open and honest manner, their perceptions change to a more equal level. This may need to be processed in front of a counselor so that it can remain a safe environment for change to occur.

The person in a victim character defect has rigid expectations/rules for their actions and no expectations/rules for their offenders' actions. Of course if the person is in physical danger they must halt the immediate threat by removing themselves and seek help from professionals. It is common for the person to need to build self confidence in order to take charge of their own lives before freeing themselves from the offender. This confidence is developed by lessening the rigid expectations we have for ourselves, and demonstrating self-nurturing behaviors. This course of action is necessary to build a strong support system in recovery through using sponsors, counselors and other mentors in Twelve Step recovery. Especially if you are a woman, these support people should be of the same gender, because more women tend to get into victim relationships than men. By acknowledging that we have the same rights as others to make change we open the door for standing up for ourselves. We then begin to place realistic expectations on those who have offended us, holding them accountable for their actions. We do this by developing realistic expectations/rules on how they should treat us and if they don't, we have a plan to get to safety.

These factors are built from the basic principle: "Do unto others as you would have them do unto you." I am not here to promote my set of beliefs onto others. I am simply stating that this is the most logical and simplest explanation of how the program assists us in changing behavior. Isolators' character defects being halted present a dilemma for those individuals. Building new relationships and activities with others to replace those isolating behaviors is the goal. Activities to do with other people are sometimes similar, but you are sharing them with others. It can even be difficult for people who haven't developed casual conversation skills, but these skills are developed by trying them out. Playing board games or cards with friends in recovery can be an ice breaker for idle conversation. Taking a class at a community college can be another outlet by interacting with others in study groups. Another may be connecting with others through email, Facebook or other social networks for interaction with family and friends; or joining a home group at a Twelve Step meeting. A home group is a Twelve Step meeting that you attend regularly and it may include providing service work. Finding a hobby that you can do with others is another possibility. One may join a gym and have a workout partner. At first we all feel awkward in taking risks, that's why doing them with others who are also new in recovery can make things a little more comfortable.

Self-esteem, the bi-product of our actions, is guided by our expectations in relationships. Don't forget that it is common for character defects to re-occur in our lives. Our worst character defects resurface when we are fearful. Social environment has a lot to do with our actions on this level. My conduct is perfectly acceptable if I surround myself with others who behave the same way I do. Just think back to playgrounds and playmates. Hanging around the same friends and bars, I'm going to revert to the same behavior. That's why we need to develop a peer group that comes from those Twelve Step meetings. We all share the same expectations of ourselves. I get smarter when I hang around other people who are acting smart about their lives. If I improve the quality of my lifestyle, the quantity of recovery will also last. Remember: by improving the quality of my life, I am getting closer to being able to have relationships where both parties have equal value.

This Step does not erase our individuality. We are addicts and we never get rid of that. We have a uniqueness of our style of living that sets us apart from others. I call this creativity and inspiration of living. We not only appreciate our own unique qualities, but the unique qualities others have in their relationships with us. My biggest fear in Step Seven was that if I worked through my character defects, there wouldn't be anything left. I was afraid I might have become just one big character defect. But that wasn't the case. After Step Seven, we no longer have to live a lifestyle based on fear. Without fear in unconditional relationships, we not only can embrace our newfound intimacy, but embrace life in general and all that it has to offer us on a daily basis.

The process we are outlining is a simple lifestyle guide. We don't need to live by anyone else's expectation or value system. We have our own. Most people are good, social-minded human beings and we gradually drift toward making change once we become aware of the impact it has on ourselves and others.

A woman once asked Benjamin Franklin how long it would take him to resolve all of his character defects. He didn't respond until the next night. At that time he said: 'I thought about your question and the answer I came up with was 35 years.' He continued, 'I think once I've completed the task of removing character defects, I would have to begin all over again to work on an entirely new set of defects I would have acquired while working on the old ones.'

In recognition that I have worked Step Seven, it isn't the weight of removing all my character defects, but the understanding that I have the skills now to work through any of my character defects. We can never do this Step perfectly or permanently remove our character defects. They can always raise their ugly head another time in our lives. The God of my understanding has lifted the burden of a life of being a hostage in my relationships through my need to be in control or in being controlled by others. I have the ability to choose today, to either act in accordance to my values, or in some cases not act at all.

These skills we have gained through Steps Six and Seven give us the ability to warrant off potential relapse or in developing another type of addiction. They have been key skills in addressing issues of procrastination and other roadblocks that take action in our lives. This recipe of self-accountability is stating my ability to make changes in myself and remain teachable and accessible in my relationships with others.

Having these new skills to my disposal, I then can take the final steps to my freedom and personal realization through Step Eight and Step Nine.

Step Eight

Made a list of people we had harmed, and became willing to make amends to them all.

After working through Step Seven, we began the journey of self-change and came to acknowledge the value of being part of society again. In building relationships with people who have been damaged by our actions, it is essential that we examine what effects our behavior has had on others.

Our fear can come up for us in beginning this Step. We may project the outcome being received with warm reception from others. We may project the worst scenario occurring with retaliation and rejection. We need to consider that we have no idea what the outcome will be until we complete the task at hand. We have prepared ourselves through the earlier work on the Steps with the support of people in the program. This new effort in Step Eight and Step Nine is a bridge into our relationship with those who have been impacted by our addiction. We are treading on unknown waters here. So, we must curb ourselves from our projections and simply take the next Step at hand, which is writing down our list of people whom we have harmed.

Using our Fourth Step and Sixth Step inventories, we look at not only what our actions were but how they affected others. We see the impact that our character defects had on others around us and the harm it had caused. We stopped the behavior which was causing harm to others in Steps Six and Seven, but in order to complete the cycle of amends we must recognize what impact our actions had on others. Our actions had a direct or indirect effect on others around us, so to commit ourselves to this new direction in our lives we must be set free of any obligations that hold us to the past. The damage we may have caused others is the last remaining hold our past has on our lives. Our guilt, shame and resentments will cause personal torment and keep us locked into the past.

Our goal in Steps Eight and Nine is to release us from the emotions and scars that bind us to the past so that we can live in the present. We know today that the fabric that binds us in our relationships with others is also the force that heals us. I have the task of disconnecting myself from those past deeds so that the same energy I use in my life today can be used for my well-being.

Step Eight uses a list of those we had harmed. The word harm refers to any damage done to a person. This may be physical, emotional, mental or spiritual abuse. I have to recognize that my actions, or the lack of, may have invoked a response from another person. My responsibility lies where my character defects have caused damage to others or myself. It may have been causing property damage, stealing something, or verbal abuse causing victimization of another person. Whatever my excuses were for doing it doesn't matter; it was my actions that caused the damage. Indirectly or directly any time someone was hurt due to my actions, I am responsible.

Most of us have told our loved ones whom we have hurt, "I am sorry" a hundred times, and they were empty words while we were acting out of our addictions. Another part of this Step is preparation for action in "willingness to make amends to them all." Many of us were living in a way that we would never have to be accountable for change. This was done through our offender behaviors as a result of our actions or lack of, and others were hurt; being victimized and not knowing a way out; or through isolating behaviors by not being available. We have the opportunity to close a chapter in our lives that has been lurking in the dark confines of our minds. With the support of our sponsors, counselors, or mentors in recovery we are prepared to make this inventory.

We need to break down our Eighth Step inventory into three sections: offender patterns, victim patterns and isolating patterns of behavior. Dealing with our offender patterns, we must determine the effects it had on those around us. This section addresses the addict with entitlement issues which were self-serving and created a pattern of dominance in their personal relationships. Often we have justified our actions and that has blocked us from seeing our part.

We may have never seen ourselves as an offender in our relationships, but more than often most addicts have a large list of people that they had harmed as a result of their character defects/actions. We see that the energy we supplied to our addictions took away from the time and energy that was for our family and closest friends. To assume responsibility for our side in our relationships with others is the task at hand. We make no justification if it was deserved or not. We see through the self-centered actions of our character defects, but we hadn't stopped to look at what impact our actions had on others. This is a time to take a closer look.

In examining our actions when we were under the influence of substances, which lowered our inhibitions, we were probably a lot more abusive toward others. Our repeated irresponsibility for our actions, or lack of, placed responsibilities for others to carry the workload of our lives. When family members gave us monetary, emotional and physical care of our needs, that cost of their energy was harm done to them. We need to be thorough in this area because it is one of the hardest for us to look at, that we became a burden to others. There are people we had hurt, but we were also victims. We need to get out of the blame game and if we are going to get better, we have to recognize our own part in the interaction. We need to break down what our responsibility was in that interaction and what was theirs to complete our inventory in the offender category. When we get to our list on the victim category, we may have to add how we were harmed. By reviewing our list with our sponsor, counselor or other mentors, our perspective may change.

Resentment is an area that is necessary to address in our amends process. Our resentments have been fortified over the years turning into walls that we thought could never be taken down. This process of placing them on our list is the beginning to dismantle that wall. Our reasons may be justified in our minds, but what these resentments are doing is giving others free rent in our heads. Even if you feel you are not ready to forgive them it is important to put it on your list of amends. In writing out our resentments and going over them with a sponsor or counselor we may gain a different perspective of the problem.

By addressing the insensitivity in our relationships with others in the past, working the Eighth Step brings further confirmation to our current changing lifestyle. As we change our perception of our own values, our expectations of how we should act become closer to how we perceive others around us should act. This lessens the expectations we have for others to a more realistic fashion and brings up our expectations on how we should treat others. This brings humility and balance in our relationships with others. It helps us to 'bring up the margins' and adjust our expectations of ourselves.

The other side of this list is where we had been victimized by others. We identify those who have caused us wrong and recognize that we have the need to heal those emotional wounds. This doesn't mean we are going to leave ourselves open to being violated again by them. We need to allow ourselves to move on from those past abusive relationships into healthy ones in recovery.

When looking at our victim patterns, we need to examine the impact it had on our lives and how it dwindled our self-esteem, creating a self-destructive cycle in our lives. Yes, we need to break down those relationships of people who harmed us to see what part we played in it. It may have been because we were intoxicated and not thinking clearly which put us in harm's way. That realization is a further understanding of our addictions. Often we see women identified as being a victim more often than men. Yes, we address physical capability to protect oneself as part of the characteristic that fuels victimization. Thus women, more often than not, have less capability to protect themselves than a man does.

Often victims who have been in an abusive relationship need to examine their part, why they stayed, and what impact staying in the relationship had on them and others. We need to commit in writing about being a victim as much as being an offender. Often when we have been in the victim role, we don't pay much attention to the rigid expectations we had for ourselves or to the very few expectations we had for the offender in our lives. Giving time to review these issues on paper, and with your sponsor or counselor, will help you to recognize your value as a person in recovery. We learned that the expectations in our relationships with others need to change. Becoming aware of our victimization patterns through working the Eighth Step brings further confirmation to our now changing lifestyle. Again, we are changing the perception of our values which changes our expectations on how others should act toward us. This is a way of generating a healthy self-esteem.

Often the offender has left a trace of themselves in the emotional scaring of the person who has been victimized through physical, mental or sexual abuse. Often I have talked with victims suffering from post-traumatic stress. They state that when someone triggers the emotions of the trauma causing it to surge back up in their lives, they are often plagued with feelings of shame, and feeling less than others. Being aware of the impact that the perpetrator had on you and writing it in your list is necessary to start to redefine yourself in recovery. We will have the opportunity in Step Nine to explore this further in our personal healing.

Over the years in working with women in domestic violence, the majority of women who went into shelters went back into the same domestic violence situation they came from. Often we struggled to say that they needed to have higher expectations on how their partners treated them. It wasn't until they lessened the hard expectations they had of themselves and started to develop self-care, that they were able to hold their partners accountable for their behavior towards them. This brings us into balance in our relationships with others.

If an individual took care of someone else's needs while ignoring their own, this should also go into their amends list. This was creating victimization in their life. This characteristic is better known as co-dependency and may have caused tremendous pain and conflict in the recovering persons' life.

When I was working with the Navajo Nation, there was an ancient ritual which made a lot of sense to me. There was a ceremony that they did in a dry Sweat Lodge. They made a list of people whom they had helped in their lives, or gave energy to. During the ceremony they asked for that energy back into their lives which they had given to others as it was no longer needed for their personal growth. In the ritual, I was told by individuals who participated in the ceremony, they felt the energy coming back into their bodies through their heads. The negative energy that was theirs, which was made up of unmet expectations and unresolved problems, left their body through their feet and went back into the earth as another form.

So by making a list of people to whom we have given our energy, being through abuse or where others may have victimized us, we are releasing the negative energy that has been built in our lives. This unresolved trauma has kept us in the past.

Being victims of circumstance, the writer must list how their loss, trauma or other circumstances have affected their life and those closest to them. This gives the writer a chance to think outside of the box that they felt locked in. An example would be a person with chronic pain who has had unrelenting suffering, and they lash out at loved ones. This is understandable, but is important for the writer to be responsible for their actions. Even though they have no control over what happened to them, they are still responsible for how their actions affect others. Their list should also encompass a voice to their unresolved grief or trauma. This gives us an opportunity to share our pain with others, bringing us closer to a resolution.

I worked with a woman who was a rape victim ten years prior. Her perpetrator broke into her home and raped and beat her so badly she required hospitalization. He told her he would be back again. For ten years she drank to suppress her trauma, and slept underneath that same bed every night out of fear of him returning. Her release from her alcoholism ten years later gave her the freedom to move on from the prison inside that confined her.

The next list is on patterns of isolation and how that behavior had affected themselves and those around them. For example, the addict might have avoided contact with family because of their abuse of substance/behavior. The families respond with fear when information is unavailable about the loved one. The binger/isolators' sole confidant is their addiction. This form of isolation is of a spirit that is totally empty because no one knows who they really are, thus harming themselves.

We will see victim, offender and isolation patterns surface in our character defects through looking at the damage done to others and ourselves. We begin by putting pen to paper again, but this time we look at how our addictions and behavior affected those around us. We start again to create awareness of the actions needed to heal our relationships.

We are re-living these past experiences in our lives to bring closure to them. This fits in context to offender character defects when we affected others; or to victim character defects when we affected ourselves and others; and isolating character defects and what impact it had on ourselves and others. There were circumstances caused by our actions in which the damage can never be undone, and there are people we have listed that are no longer alive for them to hear our amends. Our purpose here is to set the tone for willingness to change and awareness of our actions. Although Step Eight isn't the final conclusion of the process, it is part of the necessary awareness to move into action in Step Nine. Find a safe place to process this Step and begin. Again, having your Fourth Step and Sixth Step inventories present can be helpful in putting your list together. Remember, this is how our behaviors, through acting out our character defects or victim, offender or isolating patterns, have affected others or ourselves. The following is a way that we present you can review most of these relationships:

Relationships with family: In what ways have I been in a pattern of a victim, offender or isolator in my relationships with family; or what ways have I disassociated or isolated myself in my responsibilities in being part of my family?

Relationships with friends and acquaintances: Is my relationship with old and new friends, either close or casual, acting out a pattern of being a victim, offender or isolator?

Relationships in our physical needs: Have I been self-destructive in taking care of my health? Have I neglected my nutritional needs and diet, my exercise, and my dental and medical needs?

Relationships based on Sexuality: Is our sense of identity in our victim, offender or isolator relationships related to our sexual behavior? This may be through our pursuit of a sexual partner and involvement in any sexual relationships, with our consent or through violation. It depends on our ability to provide for our partners needs and their willingness to provide for ours. Have we dismissed our sexual needs by not pursuing any sexual relationships due to unresolved conflicts?

Relationships based on Society: Is our sense of identity based on our victim, offender or isolation from relationships within society: on the job, in school, or involvement with probation or the criminal system? Have I intimidated people, or been the victim of intimidation? Do I have prejudices or single out individuals due to their race, color of their skin, age, sexual preference, weight, religious beliefs or gender? Have I been open to learning about my own cultural traditions that were part of my heritage?

Relationships in Public: Is our sense of identity based on our victim, offender or isolation from interactions with others in public areas, such as restaurants, bars, grocery stores, movie theaters or on the road, through road rage or reckless driving, etc.?

Relationships based on Spirituality: Is our sense of identity in context to our spiritual beliefs and practices? Have we accused others of being morally wrong because their religious beliefs are not the same as our own? Are we in a victim pattern because of our religious upbringing, feeling guilty about our actions and judging ourselves accordingly; or relying on a spiritual guide for approval for any good feelings we have about ourselves? Have I withdrawn from those religious/spiritual ties out of avoidance of unresolved conflict?

We need to take at least a week or two to write down every aspect of how our behavior hurt those we have touched in our lives. (If you don't have a week, do what you can and plan to do the Step more thoroughly, later.) Either way, it is important to notify your sponsor, counselor or other mentors that you are making the list. Do it in chronological order. In most cases, the list will be filled with names of immediate family members, sometimes co-workers and even acquaintances. Write down the names of people you hurt even if they are dead or are otherwise unavailable to make amends to. The list also involves people, institutions and places. We look at how our behavior has affected everyone around us.

Often when writing out this Step we become guilt ridden over our behavior and jump into making amends before we've done the preparation. **Don't do this!** It could cause serious damage to others. After the list is completed, read through it several times to see how you have written down the incidents involved. Do you claim responsibility for your actions? Be very detailed so that you can clearly understand the impact your behavior had on the people you have listed. What was their reaction to the situation at the time? Leave plenty of blank space. You'll need to write more as you conclude your Ninth Step. Don't forget to write about the times you harmed your own self through negative thinking or self-talk, or other self-destructive behaviors. Write down everything you can think of that may have caused harm to others. This needs to be done as objectively as possible. After you have completed the written portion of the Eighth Step, go over it with your sponsor or counselor. The purpose is to get feedback from an outside source that can look at it in a realistic and objective manner. After getting the feedback, do what is suggested before processing the Ninth Step.

As we write our list it becomes evident that we are responsible for a lot of damage in our relationships with others. It becomes overwhelming, and in our ability to face this on our own we may project possibilities of how we intend on doing the amends. However, it is strongly suggested to keep in touch with a sponsor and wait and review the outcome of your Eighth Step before taking any action on making amends. It is common for people to want to go through this process quickly because it is bringing up strong feelings for the writer. If we don't carefully plan out our amends with our sponsor or counselor we could do more harm than good. Willingness is the key here, following direction: first Step Eight, then Step Nine. Our willingness to use the resources of the program, sponsors, Twelve Step group, counselors and spiritual advisors, will help us strengthen our damaged relationships with those we are closest to.

Once you have completed a thorough inventory, you are now prepared to move onto Step Nine.

Step Nine

Made direct amends to such people wherever possible, except when to do so would injure them or others.

In Step Eight we became aware of what impact our actions had on those around us. We gained insight to our victim, offender and isolating character defects and the harm it had done to others and ourselves. This new awareness transported us from a place of being stuck to a place of transition in ourselves and in our relationships with others. Now in Step Nine we take action in making our amends to attempt to heal the wounds we caused by our character defects.

We are faced with fear usually in our first few steps of embarking on this effort. We have made tremendous and miraculous changes as a result of the work we have done before this. The work we have done previously has set the stage for our actions in Step Nine. In Steps Four and Five we took a comprehensive look at our lives and shared everything with one human being. In Steps Six and Seven we halted our destructive path of our character defects and opened the doorway to unconditional relationships with others. This paves the way for working skills of practicing humility in our relationships with others. We now approach our actions of working Step Nine with the spiritual principles we have learned. In working the Steps we have found humility, honesty and sincerity. We are at this phase of our recovery to make direct amends, not because we are told to, but because we see in our hearts that our obligation to make things right is at hand.

We approach this Step in the beginning of each amends with asking for guidance and strength from our loving God, in how He may portray Himself in our lives. Remember, the first word in the First Step is "We" having at our disposal our sponsor, counselors, and others in Twelve Step recovery. We work on each amends individually so that we may prepare for taking action in this Step. Bouncing off what our plans of amends are to our mentors in recovery, we will find encouragement and guidance. It is important to use someone else's judgment in monitoring our progress here because often we lose perspective.

We don't realize that by sharing this information we could hurt others in the process. For instance, I have seen men jump into talking with their wives about a short-lived affair because they thought it would help them build trust and honesty into their marital relationships. It often had the reverse effect. Many times when a spouse is confronted with a partner's improprieties, the spouse asks for details in an attempt to develop some sense of control of the situation. While the person confessing might not see the situation as so bad because it happened several years ago, the spouse is just finding out about it in the present. The spouse is feeling the impact as if it just happened. The partner, feeling that providing the details is necessary to relieve himself of the guilt, does so. But that only causes further trauma for the spouse.

I am not here to recommend any specific or standard method of determining if amends should be indirect or direct. I only suggest that the recovering individual gets specific feedback from a counselor or sponsor who knows of the situation and them. When making direct amends is determined, weighing out the best method to lessen the impact on the receiver should be considered. The avenue of making amends may require being in counseling with their partner to build credibility about their sincerity to change. Then perhaps it would be possible to make those amends with supervision of a counselor/sponsor to assist in damage control. Indirect amends also should be reviewed by an objective third party, as in making direct amends. An indirect amends may be showing appreciation for their partner, and obviously stopping the behavior that you are making amends for. In some cases ending a relationship where the wreckage has been unresolvable may be the appropriate amends, so as not to continue to cause harm to them. This is certainly only one example of a particular type of amends. This process should be followed through with all amends we are about to make.

Making amends to those who we have resentments towards eases us from the energy we give in these relationships which are destructive to us. Many of us have been stuck behind our resentments feeling like we have been in a prison with no freedom from the conflict. We may feel conflicted and tormented by the issue in our own heads, but they may not be affected at all. The purpose is to evict the resentment from our heads where we have been giving it free rent.

Taking the power away from these relationships will help us balance out our personal lives. We tend to place unrealistic, rigid expectations on those we harbor resentments towards. The more power we give them the less human they become in our minds. We may begin to demonize them which leave those relationships irresolvable. We need to take time out and imagine them being loved and cared for by another person. Imagine them being hugged by a loved one or having a warm evening with family next to their Christmas tree on Christmas Day. We may pray for them that they receive all those things we would like for ourselves.

By talking with your sponsor, counselor or others in Twelve Step recovery, you might find a method of approaching your Ninth Step work. It may involve having a third party mediate the situation, or if you feel comfortable enough without fear of retaliation, approach them yourself. Some people we have resentments towards are unavailable possibly because of being deceased or it is not safe or appropriate for us to have direct contact. Yes, it is our perception that these individuals hurt us in some way, and that has turned into resentment. In some cases our resentments were instilled by our self-centeredness and by discussing the matter with others we may recognize it was about us, not them.

There are some resentments we may find no resolution to, no matter who we talk with. In these circumstances turning our resentment over to our Higher Power will offer us a detachment from our resentment. That particular resentment could resurface, but using this method will keep it at bay. Often resentments leave the person feeling that something was taken from them. I have suggested to someone suffering like this to change their thoughts and get into the present. They may do this by reading a daily meditation book, making a simple prayer or a gratitude list, etc. We have grown accustom to thinking, "I am scarred because of the abusive childhood and nothing good will come to me." *Change this to "I am in recovery,* (list several assets here), *and abundance and prosperity will fill my life today. Opportunity for new insights and awareness will come to me today through my relationships with others."* Say this until you believe it at least a few times a day. Sometimes I have to change my thinking to change how I feel.

We have the need to make amends to others who have also harmed us. We must set aside our resentments and focus on the task at hand. We must approach these amends with assistance, so as not to react and end up in a verbal conflict with them. We talk with sponsors and mentors in recovery about what our intentions are and what we intend to say. Even though we may have been hurt by this person we are responsible at this time for being accountable for our actions. Remaining objective is the task at hand while in our amends process with them. We must separate our hurt feelings and go into this objectively. If we are not prepared to do this it would be better to put it off until we have done further work on ourselves.

The benefit of this amends is to take your energy back from this relationship so that you may use it in a more constructive way in your life. By sitting down with them, our honesty might bring out warmth in them that we didn't expect. It may take time for this effort to work; those feelings take time to resolve. If we have made our best effort and shook their hands walking away, we have started a process of change.

Amends serve as a learning process for people in recovery. This Step is not just to heal their relationships, but to prepare them to digest what impact their actions actually had on others. Not until a person has walked in the footsteps of the one they harmed can he or she truly learn from the experience. We listen to the impact our behavior had on the loved ones or the person they affected. Making a face-to-face amends, when appropriate, can be a healthy and deeply healing part of recovery. But it cannot be done haphazardly. Ask to schedule a sit-down with the person. Listen and respect their wishes if they tell you they are not emotionally ready for that interaction in their life. Perhaps they will say they will never be ready and that must also be respected. If however, the injured party has set up a time to discuss the amends with you, ask them where they would like to meet. This is your amends, but it is the injured party who needs to feel as comfortable as possible.

You may start the conversation with how long you have been in recovery and you must show sincerity. Make sure you have in memory what you want to say. Discussing your behavior with the person and asking how it affected them is the other part of amends. Listen to the injured person's experience without interruption or justification; apologize and then leave in a comfortable fashion. This all helps us to get closure for ourselves, and may give us the ability to continue with the relationship. We now have a different outlook on the experience for ourselves.

We may or may not have been able to affect the perception or depth of the pain experienced by the person we hurt, but we have made the effort. Pain does not end by my time clock. It must heal in a way that the injured party can accept on his or her own. Making amends will take time and lots of thought. Be aware that we have no way of knowing how people will react to our amends. Some may walk away being upset or angry, each person who we have affected has their own way of dealing with the amends. We may have humbly asked forgiveness from the other party and if it was not acknowledged, we must go on at this point realizing that we did the best we could.

There are those in our lives who are closest to us that probably have been hurt the most by our actions. In some cases there is no complete amends that can be made, an example being from a childhood lost because of a parent's addiction or to a death of someone due to our actions or negligence due to our addictions. There are many of us that will live with guilt that no human being can relieve; in that case we turn to our Higher Power, a loving God to help us to find forgiveness.

There are those things in my life that I live with, that I am aware I cannot undo. My strength for change has come from those lessons and has kept me teachable in my life in recovery. Many of us have taken the pain of addictions and turned it into hope, unbridled dedication to helping others in recovery. We have to turn the outcome over to our Higher Power and give our best shot at making amends.

Just select people and circumstances that seem to have the biggest priority in your mind. Get through one amends at a time. If we examine our motives before making the amends and find we are truly sincere; and we are willing to make restitution for the damage we have done, then we are ready.

Use your written Eighth Step list and make a journal, filling in now where you left it blank for the Ninth Step. Write down what the people you made amends to, told you about the impact they saw your behavior had on them. The purpose of this is to reinforce your awareness of the effect your behavior had on others. Remember you must gage your behavior as offensive, not necessarily by your perspective, but of that of those you offended.

This is truly a sobering experience and one you'll need time to process. Talk with your counselor, sponsor or mentor in program about the experience. Keep your priorities in place. Amends is the catalyst for our reconciliation in relationships. This process of amends helps us begin to negotiate an ongoing relationship that we can co-exist in a relationship in the moment. It also brings us to a place where we can embrace the personal relationship we have with utmost respect for the person involved.

It may seem that some of our amends are trivial while other issues may seem overwhelming. It is the willingness to come forward with our accountability that is the measurable force. Many of our amends will be directed towards close friends and family. The people we hurt most were those closest to us. A lot of the time we dumped our emotional wreckage on them, we certainly weren't available to them for their needs. Our self-centeredness drained them of personal resources in their own lives and inflicted chaos and pain. Our words may not mean much to them because they had heard our apologies so many times before. Our measure of amends may be seen in the changes we have made through taking responsibility for our actions, and the interest to be involved in their lives. The loss of communication and trust were two aspects that prevailed in our addictions and we must attempt to build these back into our relationships. Openly talking with them about our emotional needs and listening to theirs is crucial.

Walking our talk is the measure of true change. I may have been acting out in my addictions for many years and a ten minute amends doesn't set it right. It is through our future actions that will show our intentions on truly making change in the relationship. Being available for their support, being at special occasions, birthdays, anniversaries, etc., is showing true interest in their lives. Our actions in the past shut us off from building relationships with others. Our intent is to build relationships in the positive light of recovery. These aren't just words; it's our actions that count. Restitution in these relationships may be on a monetary accountability by paying back money we borrowed from family and friends; or taking care of our legal issues which we have put off. We are changing the attitude that 'I will deal with it when they catch me.' We are growing into a respectable, responsible partner to those around us as part of our recovery.

Some of the restitution is legal, recognizing we have an obligation to take care of our past wreckage which may require legal counsel. Working with a sponsor, counselor and others in Twelve Step recovery, I have seen countless individuals who had lived in the shadows of addiction coming forward and becoming productive members of our society.

Restitution for our behaviors is always part of our actions of the Ninth Step, because we are building back our sense of value in our relationships with others. Through this method we gain humility for our actions. Restitution may mean time, commitment and/or financial reimbursement. We may have gotten an enormous debt that had in itself kept us feeling overwhelmed and immobilized to do anything about it. We may need financial guidance from professionals to resolve this issue. We may have had years of not paying our bills, letting them go until they shut off the lights.

Our restitution is learning to live within our means and being financially accountable to others. As part of our amends we contact our debtors and make a financial plan to take care of our bills; we may have to maintain a tight budget. We may have a large portion of our checks taken out due to a divorce and child support. Our attitudes about those responsibilities also have to change as part of our personal recovery. Yes, it hurts financially and it weighs heavily on our minds, we must do our best and not let it become another prison to us. Our attitude of recovery is essential for our outlook of life to be positive. We are taking responsibility for our actions which is demonstrated by what changes we continue with in our new found life in recovery. Possibly one of the most beneficial forms of restitution is building hope back in our lives again. Living without the chains of addiction allows us to become part of society again, and our continued actions build positive karma in our lives.

In circumstances where our amends may hurt someone else, it often is better to talk with a sponsor or counselor to come up with indirect amends, ones that will give the person sufficient satisfaction that they have made amends, but ones also that will not further traumatize the victim.

I was sponsoring a man who had just completed his Eighth Step. Without talking to me, and while he was in an inpatient facility, he went home on pass and knocked on the door of his parents' neighbor. He introduced himself as being in recovery. He had heard that the neighbor also was in a Twelve Step program. The neighbor congratulated him for being in recovery and told him he would be glad to take him to a meeting sometime. He then told the man that he was there to present an amends. He said that he had broken into the neighbor's house four years earlier and had stolen some of his guns. The neighbor called the police and had him arrested. He ended up serving two and a half years in prison as a result of that amends and he blamed the Twelve Step program for his predicament. I reminded him that he had been informed to let his sponsor review his amends before he acted on them, and he hadn't done that. If I were informed of the circumstances I probably would have recommended legal counsel before proceeding any further.

Perhaps it would have been better to complete the amends by figuring out what the guns had been worth and slipping the money under the neighbor's door. Another part of that amends could have been to talk to others who had their houses broken into and gain a sense of how they felt violated. In finding out what it felt like to them, he would have gained a better understanding of the impact he had made on the neighbor.

In other circumstances where we had resentments towards someone and ridiculed them behind their backs, the harm it caused was real but for us to bring this to their attention would harm them. Indirect amends would be more appropriate by stopping the behavior and showing a more positive interaction with others.

It still is important to follow through the process of making amends on our side when trying to make amends in a relationship involving an individual who has died, or is unavailable to make amends. Some ways to make amends to a person who has died is by discussing what happened with a counselor, writing out what happened or even going to the gravesite. Some people have written amends on a piece of paper that they attached to a helium balloon and then sent it skyward. Others have decided to present amends to loved ones of the deceased.

There may be people that we injured who we didn't know and have no way of making direct amends. We may call this indirect amends for our actions.

One example is there were people that were harmed by my actions that I had not personally known. I was a street kid in a major city with my priority being my alcohol and substance abuse over any other relationships. I participated in doing volunteer work, at community agencies and nonprofit programs for many years, and still do.

This type of restitution can be healing to a community and to the individual. Indirect amends can come in other forms by showing love and unconditional support for others in the community.

There may be people on our list that have moved to another part of the country. If face to face isn't possible, we could simply get a hold of them by phone or internet. Preferably, it would be better to have some type of dialogue with them. Keep an open attitude and promptly make the effort to give your amends if they become available.

The effort to deal with the harm we caused others in our past brings us to a place of freedom from our unrealistic expectations in our present relationships. We have dealt with the water under the bridge, now we are ready to sail on. We have placed the burden of responsibility on our own shoulders which shows credibility and strength in our relationships with others. (We have changed our liabilities into assets.) We are able to affirm our value and others', in unconditional relationships today. What this process does is gives the recovering person the opportunity to come to a point of acceptance for his or her part of the interaction, and then lets that person move on with grace.

We have addressed making amends due to our offender behaviors. It is essential to address how to make amends to ourselves due to being victims in our lives. Yes we were hurt by others and by our own behavior in the past. Now I want to point out, it is about making amends to ourselves, not the perpetrator who has offended us. By doing this, we are not allowing them back in our lives to perpetrate us again. We are reconciling our relationships with others through this Step to allow ourselves to heal and move on.

Our mission in Step Nine, in dealing with our victimization, is about allowing us to heal our emotional wounds which we have covered through the use of our addictions. The amends we are making here is to ourselves. Depending on the circumstances, contact with the offender may not be necessary unless we have a continued relationship with him/her. In those circumstances it is about setting boundaries with the offender in our life, so not to be a continued source of victimization. We often can change our relationship with the offender to an unconditional relationship in recovery. Processing this decision should be done with the support of a sponsor or counselor. The pain and turmoil that have been left in these wounds need to be cleaned to allow it to heal. First, we must feel safe to begin this process. We surround ourselves with the healing relationships we find in the rooms of recovery, our sponsors, counselors, loved ones, etc. We address each issue individually and look through deep introspection what message was left in the wound within us. Often there was dwindled self-esteem, and often the victim feels that something was taken from them by the offender. This releases us from the prison of the silence that was left in our emotional wounds, which were cemented in with shame and dishonor.

An example is, in my childhood I was bullied through middle adolescence. I lived with shame about who I was and it affected my ability to grow. I thought of myself as stupid and useless which was instilled by those offenders who had perpetrated me. I found in recovery that I was an intelligent, caring human being. My deep emotional pain that I endured became strength to show love, care and compassion for others in recovery. I changed those words that kept me a prisoner, and transformed them into a deeper appreciation and insight into others and myself.

The offender is given power to control our lives well after the trauma has been left. We clean out the wound and take our power back from the perpetrator in our lives, and then fill our lives with healing activities and thoughts to replace the negative. Once we define what that was, we begin a restoration process of ourselves, and we fill that emotional wound with the love and nurturing we have found in recovery.

With some scarring from being victimized, we may have these memories triggered to reoccur in our lives. Being involved in counseling may offer the tools to equip a person to restore balance back into their lives. Quite simply, when the past interferes with living in the present it is time to seek outside assistance.

Other victimizations may include losses in our lives from relationships, careers, chronic pain, physical disability or other factors. Writing out and sharing these as part of our list to sponsors, counselors and others in recovery is part of the Ninth Step. The addict gets stuck behind their grief, not allowing it to pass by using their addiction to numb their pain. Often in our process of grief we find ourselves delving into self-pity. Self-pity could be known as the first stage of grieving; we are experiencing the loss of something or someone in our lives but we are not sharing it with anyone else. That is why it is called "self-pity", or otherwise it would be known as self-grieving. The issue is that a person cannot come to acceptance of a loss without processing the grief with someone else. Similar to using pall bearers at a funeral, we need a handful of people to assist us in letting go of our loss. By processing these areas of our lives with other people we come to acceptance. For example, through sharing our grief with others, we get beyond the pain and find joy in our loved one's memory. Another example is a person with chronic pain or a physical disability. By sharing their losses with others it brings them to a place of acceptance. Through sharing with others they can effectively chart a new direction with hope.

It is however important to recognize that grieving over a loss has a beginning, middle and end to the process. Often you may find the person sharing their pain once and then shutting down the process, expecting them-selves to move on. The person ends up feeling conflicted over their unresolved grief. It takes time for a person to transition through the stages of coming to terms with their grief. When working for the Apache people, they would visit the grave site of a family member once a week for a year as part of their tribal traditions.

In being a victim of circumstances which was perpetuated by our addictions, it is necessary to make amends to those that we have harmed due to our actions. We lived in our addictions, alienating those that loved us, or projecting the lack of satisfaction in our lives onto them. In making amends we recognize that the pain we inflicted onto others was not warranted. We may not have seen ourselves as being offenders, but the only way we can be set free from our addictions is to set free those that we affected. The methods and approaches to making those amends were listed earlier in this chapter.

The addict in isolating/binge character defects must recognize the impact their behavior has had on others. Both victimization of themselves and others has occurred from their isolation. A big part of their amends is willingness to get involved in relationships with others. This effort can trigger anxiety for some because of the isolation they had lived in. Certainly direct amends is still an important part of this process. For example, a family may live with dread out of fear of potential harm that their alcoholic/addict could be facing, because there is no contact from them. In other cases, the concealment of their addiction brings forth the need for honesty about its severity.

Let's not forget to write about hurting ourselves. But the question then is: What nurturing behaviors can I construct to make amends to myself? It totally depends on the individual. We make restitution to ourselves through nurturing care and loving attention, and we begin to heal. Certainly lessening the expectations of ourselves is part of that restitution. I have seen people take time for self-care simply through going to the dentist, joining a health club, listening to their favorite music or reading a book for their enjoyment. It may be going back to school or taking time out for a hobby that I haven't allowed for myself. It could simply be taking time to play Sudoku when I have a few minutes.

Changing the rigid expectations we have had for ourselves can occur only with self-nurturing behaviors and by nurturing relationships with others. People who have victim patterns in their lives tend to feel guilty about taking time out for themselves. For those who always have to be busy doing something, because if they don't they feel guilty, it is about taking time to find things they can place in their lives that bring them joy. It is important to give themselves the gift of a life full of rewards, which can build a self-nurturing life. We have to learn to fill time with activities that bring us joy and are not just ways of killing time. Setting up activities and schedules that help us to be productive is necessary for amends to occur, because part of the amends is learning to live another way. We should fill our calendars with activities which we can participate in that support recovery. Then stick to it. Get out there in the action. To start having a social life, begin simply by going out for coffee with some of the members of the Twelve Step meeting you attend. We call it the 'meeting after the meeting'.

What this effort in making amends does is puts our talk into action. Our recovery becomes solidified in reckoning with our past relationships. This process brings home a true belief that our recovery isn't just a choice. It is our path for personal interactions with others. Step Nine takes us out of our self-centered world into a world shared by others. This act of humility brings us closer to others and brings us to an image of where we are today which we can embrace. Developing relationships with others in recovery builds self-esteem back into our lives. We walked away from this Step with a ton of less guilt and resentment towards others. We shed these garments for a new image of ourselves, being a more mature, caring, and loving individual.

Step Ten

Continued to take personal inventory and when we were wrong promptly admitted it.

Steps One through Nine assisted us to halt our addictions and restore balance back into our relationships. Our investment in our recovery through willingness, honesty, humility and clearing up the wreckage of our past has brought about a new realization of who we are today. We have built our lives surrounding the spiritual principals of the Twelve Steps of recovery.

Steps Ten, Eleven and Twelve are known as the maintenance Steps: ones we perform every day. Why do we need to proceed with this continued review of our lives? After all, we have taken pain staking effort to change the direction of our lives by sifting through our past experiences. Our efforts would be futile if we quit here, relapse is a certain danger for any of us in recovery. In our experience, those who become complacent in practicing the principals of recovery have placed themselves at risk of relapse into their addictions or into another type of addiction.

Often relapse patterns have been defined as returning to behavior patterns that were prominent during the person's addiction. These behaviors were character defects that kept our denial intact. Some people used aggressive behavior to push people away, others may have used a demanding relationship to avoid dealing with their own needs, and others may have gotten into isolating behaviors. Character defects can slip back into place like an old glove, feeling natural because they were part of our life for a long time. The Tenth Step keeps our actions in check so that we can be aware of the warning signs of these dangerous relapse patterns occurring in our lives. The person not acknowledging accountability for their actions is allowing negative energy to grow in them. They slip back into denial through their actions, which without intervention will lead into relapse.

When I was 5 years sober I was working at an agency as a counselor, where I began slipping into my old negative/intimidating behavior with my co-staff. I had been getting negative and was confronted by the entire staff. I thought at that point in time I would respond with compliance and agree with them, although I was angry about their confrontation. They suggested that I go to some outside counseling to review my actions. One of the staff members brought up that there was a positive reinforcement workshop going on this weekend and suggested I go, so I agreed. I went to the workshop, but because I was still in denial and full of resentment toward those who confronted me, my interactions at the workshop were abrupt and negative. I was kicked out of a positive reinforcement workshop because of my negative attitude at the time! I thought about my actions over the weekend. I realized that I was pointing the finger at everyone else before and remembered that when pointing a finger at someone else, there are three more fingers pointing back at me. I gained humility from that experience, insight into my disease of addiction and my character defects, realizing that they are greater than me as an individual.

Yes, we have started down the road to recovery and it is easy to stray off our course. Our personality that led us into addiction is still with us, even though our disease is in remission. Like a garden if I don't pull the weeds it can spread, killing off what I was trying to grow. Without this Tenth Step our unbridled character defects grow in us. Our half-truths, controlling behavior, resentments and unresolved conflict build walls around us, blocking us from a clear perspective. Even in long term recovery, this can turn into a deteriorating lifestyle ending in relapse and self-destructive behavior.

Let us remember that the rigid thinking of our character defects kept us locked into a life that stopped us from being teachable. Step Ten allows us to review our everyday interactions and how we are applying the principals that we have learned in recovery. Our ability to maintain unconditional relationships with others is sustained in our constant evaluation of our interactions in the present day.

Step Ten's moral inventory can be as simple as making a journal or a mental note of what I had done, right and wrong in context to my values – and promptly admitting when I was wrong. We keep appraised of our victim, offender and isolating character defects in this manner on a day in and day out basis. This side of the inventory of spontaneous amends is a check point to maintain a balance in the expectations we have for others and the expectations we have for ourselves. I have found this keeps me aware of my actions in general in my personal and social relationships. I have had bad days in recovery where my attitude was poor and I was quick with my wife. By being aware of it, I made amends for my actions. The benefit of making amends immediately after I recognize the mistake is what brings my personal values to the surface, being my expectations for my behavior and its' impact on others. This also brings out inventorying what my boundaries are in relation to the expectations I have on how others should treat me. The total purpose is keeping a balance in my relationships with others, and helping me maintain awareness of my actions.

I have often used the Tenth Step in couples counseling as a tool to lead them to a conscious state of awareness. The idea that we are going to make mistakes along the road of life is something we all can understand. I have had people in domestic violence treatment who have said: 'I am aware of my spouse's needs and her input is valuable today, but how do I know if I am starting to shift back to the old character defects of entitlement?' Like we said before, these behaviors were ingrained into our lives over a long period of time. To be concerned that they could resurface in our lives keeps us alert and teachable. The Tenth Step is the tool to keep us on the track of balanced relationships. The term I use is "unconditional relationships." We are no longer in victim, offender or isolating patterns, where we imprison ourselves or hold others hostage. To keep us out of the chains of our character defects we must follow Step Ten on a daily basis. This process gives us clear indications about the balance of expectations we have for our own behavior and our expectation of how we perceive others should act toward us.

When I am holding onto resentments, Step Ten is the place to air those feelings in our relationships. By inventorying my emotional reaction to someone's behavior, I can share my feelings with clarity to the one I'm feeling effected by. For example, in thoughtfully sharing my anger about someone's actions toward me, I may find mutual agreement in the expectations of acceptable behavior in that relationship. This allows an opportunity for exchange on both sides of the interaction. I am not going to control the outcome of any interaction with others, but I will have input into the relationship. This is part of a personal inventory having clear insight into both sides of an interaction. It eliminates confusion and the need for assumptions.

So far we have broken the Step down into: 1) Reviewing our actions in relationships with others and discussing our amends with others; and 2) Reviewing expectations of others' actions toward us and our interaction with others. This review assists us in continuing to create safe and fluid interdependent relationships. We are always changing in our relationships and in our environment. Keeping spontaneous gives us the ability to be successful and to gain the full potential of relationships.

I found that taking an inventory of my attitude at the start of the day has been essential to improving the quality of my day. I take time out and assess my daily goals, viewing over the perspective highlights of the day in a positive fashion. This effort is helpful in having a different outlook as things come to pass during the day. I may start the day out in a negative light thinking about the things that I fear most as possible outcomes. It is important to attempt to alter this view of my interaction with the world.

Starting the day with having a positive view creates new ideas, new perceptions and a new understanding of how my day will go, which will be revealed to me through my relationships with others. For example, I may think or wish that health, abundance and prosperity will build in my life today, and I may give thanks for those things. Now I can set goals that I would like to accomplish.

In starting out the day with negative thoughts, I am not able to see something good happening even if it is right in front of my face. We all have had patterns of negative thinking that have consumed us at some point in our lives. We can't change from being negative thinkers to positive thinkers overnight. I do believe, however, that overnight we can be open to the possibility of positive things coming into our lives. Negative thinking is part of my character defects, and in most cases I am saying I am in control because I can't see any good coming out of something. This attitude is a self-fulfilling prophecy. It will continue to draw further negative outcomes because the more energy I give it, the more it resurfaces in my life. I am not saying that a person can change every aspect of being a negative thinker, but I am saying that it doesn't have to be a prison. I can open the day up to positive things happening in my life.

Scheduling the time to work this Step is important. It is a good idea to set aside two periods of evaluation. 1) First thing in the morning before getting out of bed. As we mentioned earlier, it helps in the review of our attitude and direction. 2) At the end of the day when we are getting prepared for bed. Perhaps just before we brush our teeth or when we lay down is a good time to reflect what we did right and what we did wrong today. It is not just being accountable for our actions in how we affected others; it is also how we were affected by others. This is a time to look at what we did right also, giving us an "at-a-boy" pat on the back and affirm that we are on a spiritual path in recovery. If we become aware that we need to make amends to someone, we can make a mental note of it when we see the person the next time.

Some people use a Tenth Step guide to assist them in writing out this Step. Using the inventory of our relationships that we presented in the Fourth, Sixth and Eighth Steps is a way of reviewing our relationships with others:

Relationships with family: In what ways have I been in a pattern of a victim, offender or isolator in my relationships with family; or what ways have I disassociated or isolated myself in my responsibilities in being part of my family?

Relationships with friends and acquaintances: Is my relationship with old and new friends, either close or casual, acting out a pattern of being a victim, offender or isolator?

Relationships in our physical needs: Have I been self-destructive in taking care of my health? Have I neglected my nutritional needs and diet, my exercise, and my dental and medical needs?

Relationships based on Sexuality: Is our sense of identity in our victim, offender or isolator relationships related to our sexual behavior? This may be through our pursuit of a sexual partner and involvement in any sexual relationships, with our consent or through violation. It depends on our ability to provide for our partners needs and their willingness to provide for ours. Have we dismissed our sexual needs by not pursuing any sexual relationships due to unresolved conflicts?

Relationships based on Society: Is our sense of identity based on our victim, offender or isolation from relationships within society: on the job, in school, or involvement with probation or the criminal system? Have I intimidated people, or been the victim of intimidation? Do I have prejudices or single out individuals due to their race, color of their skin, age, sexual preference, weight, religious beliefs or gender? Have I been open to learning about my own cultural traditions that were part of my heritage?

Relationships in Public: Is our sense of identity based on our victim, offender or isolation from interactions with others in public areas, such as restaurants, bars, grocery stores, movie theaters or on the road, through road rage or reckless driving, etc.?

Relationships based on Spirituality: Is our sense of identity in context to our spiritual beliefs and practices? Have we accused others of being morally wrong because their religious beliefs are not the same as our own? Are we in a victim pattern because of our religious upbringing, feeling guilty about our actions and judging ourselves accordingly; or relying on a spiritual guide for approval for any good feelings we have about ourselves? Have I withdrawn from those religious/spiritual ties out of avoidance of unresolved conflict?

There are other materials available and certainly a journal is a good method of keeping track of your Tenth Step . If you found yourself having a conflict with someone, discussing how to approach the problem with your sponsor or another person is part of the Tenth Step.

As we proceed with this process we will get further indication of a need to make amends by our conscience or feedback from others of our wrong doings. That small voice inside, which is the voice of our true self, becomes awakened. We are acknowledging that we have slipped off the path of recovery and need to get back on track. With awareness comes accountability for our actions. It is amazing how effective this is in building healthy relationships with others. The response to a sincere amends is usually met with respect from the other party. But again, we are not in control of the outcome, and motives should not be set, other than to proceed for personal resolution.

We proceed courageously in continuing to build relationships with others. I realize that my self-centered values were the architect for my controlling relationships with others. We use Step Ten to correct these errors in our judgment. The program has taught me a set of spiritual principles which has brought me to a position of humility in my actions. We now move on to Step Eleven.

Step Eleven

Sought through prayer and meditation to improve our conscious contact with God, as we understood Him, praying only for knowledge of His will for us and the power to carry that out.

It is imperative that our actions in recovery remain fluid. The inflexibility of addiction did not allow us to open our eyes to the impact it was having on our lives and the lives of others. Being teachable has been a key through working the Steps and so it is important to continue this through the development of our spiritual beliefs.

Prayer is the questions we ask from our hearts, seeking the answers we need to be successful in this journey of recovery. Prayer is creating the attitude of being teachable. Our addictions were a power greater than ourselves, which created chaos in our lives. Opening the door to a positive power outside of us opens an attitude of new possibilities and inspiration in our lives. There are countless books on spiritual directions a person can take in their recovery. Step Eleven talks about the personal development of that spiritual belief which is open to any direction that inspires the recovering person.

Meditation is showing respect to our perception of God by humbly waiting for answers through silencing and opening our minds to the world, as it unfolds in our lives. We listen for the answers in our present day in and day out activities. A meditative state is a method of building stronger ties to the present moment, which is where we find our answers to our problems and prayers. Our ability to focus on the present moment is often limited to only a few minutes, then, we drift into random thought. The more we meditate the longer our concentration builds so that we fade off less into random thought. These thoughts usually consist of our past, or projection of what may come about in our future. These thoughts will trigger fear or anger which releases adrenaline being pumped into our bodies. This creates anxiety and further stress. Meditation works at exercising the brain in developing concentration so that we may stay longer in the present moment.

The more we stay in the present, we have less stress and life begins to feel more manageable. Meditating rewards the individual in development of empathy and concentration in our brain activity. This concept has been known as "Loving Gentle Kindness" in meditation circles.

Meditation can be anything that aids in silencing the mind, and brings a state of calm. We use exercise to build a healthier body. Using meditation helps to build a healthier mind. Those who believe in meditation say that if we take 20 minutes daily to meditate, it will change our thinking. Some people fear meditation because they believe it will potentially cause unhealthy things to come into them. If they have this belief, it would be to their advantage to pray, asking the God of their understanding to place a circle of protection around them during their meditation. One could also use a mantra – a word or phrase that we say in our minds when we breathe out and in. Some Christians may use the word "Jesus" on the inhalation and "Christ" on the exhalation. Others may use the universal mantra of "soo" on the inhalation and "humm" on the exhalation. Still others may choose to join a meditation group. Singing songs of inspiration has been a process used in churches for thousands of years.

Mindfulness Meditation is a concept of being in a relaxed state of consciousness. It is being in the present, aware of our sensations, feelings, thoughts, breathing and surroundings in a non-resistant, non-critical, peaceful state of mind. Like any muscles in our body, we need to exercise our mind to keep it functioning sharply. Setting a time for this activity on a daily basis is important, usually out of sight-out of mind occurs. We all should have a place set up as our personal spiritual sanctuary, be it a corner of our bedroom or a whole separate room. This space is necessary so we can prepare our attitude and posture for prayer and meditation. Some people prefer a church where there is space already set up for that purpose. Others may find their church out in nature, taking hikes and witnessing the breath taking views while practicing their prayer and meditation, feeling harmony with nature. Some people may pray on their knees or sit with their legs crossed in a yoga position. Creating a place for prayer proves the sincerity of our attitude. For my own prayer and meditation, I use a sunroom with plants and a fountain. This practice is healthful in almost every walk of life. In my experience I have seen that meditation assists in slowing down mental aging diseases such as Dementia and Alzheimer's.

Reading spiritual materials helps to gain focus. Twelve Step daily meditation books are part of the spiritual materials that aid people in recovery. Some forms of meditation have you select an image that brings tranquility in your life and as a part of meditation, has the person bring up the image of that in their own mind. I have seen individuals develop an interest in using digital cameras to record experiences through nature, family or friends. Having these photos in their computer where they can look at them easily frequently brings them a sense of spirituality that helps to calm their day.

Having a spiritual group that you share these events with is also a positive element for recovery. Some people may find this in a community church or in an organized religion. Even attending a Twelve Step meeting where the topic is on spirituality or on the Third Step helps this process. I started a group that I called SOCR – Sharing Our Creativity in Recovery. Through poetry, song or art we shared the experiences we were having that were our inspiration in recovery that day.

A lot of times it is the simple things that bring the rewards of inspiration and spiritual invigoration into our lives. Having music around that makes our hearts sing is also part of the Eleventh Step because it is aiding us to elevate our consciousness to a positive state of being. Being open to other methods helps us to change our perception of the world. We can do this through a prayer group or reading inspirational books which opens our view of the world. It always involves sharing this process in our relationships, as that is the catalyst for change to occur in our lives. The more I think I know everything there is to know about my Higher Power, the more I tend to be replacing faith with self-pride. Am I open to being a student of spirituality, discussing with others at Twelve Step meetings about their own perception of a Higher Power, without feeling threatened about my own? This open interaction challenges my beliefs and allows me to adapt those beliefs as they grow in my recovery.

Some of the most inspirational experiences have come about from someone beginning to open up to a belief in God; by trusting through blind faith in something they couldn't comprehend. A God consciousness would represent to most, a Power greater than ourselves which is beyond their understanding. This concept allows us to be open toward something we cannot fully understand. If we believe that God is a conscious being, in most cases we perceive that it is a loving God. This belief opens up a positive outlook, which changes our perception of the world.

I once took a group of men out for a spiritual retreat. While sitting around the camp fire we were talking about the issue of trusting something outside of us that we didn't understand. In the middle of the conversation someone pointed to the Big Dipper and said, "Doesn't that look like a big question mark to you?" Now, whenever I look up into the night sky, I don't see the Big Dipper, I see a big question mark.

There are certain common characteristics which are interwoven throughout all the history of man's belief in God.

For example, the Hopi Nation has a ceremony that begins with people who might be interpreted as clowns, who try to persuade their tribal members to focus on things that are against their traditions. As the day proceeds they continue to attempt to get others distracted. At the morning light the Kachina dancers come out and they focus on their traditions and tribal responsibilities. The Kachina dancers run off the clowns. This is an epic tale of good vs. bad in our spiritual and personal values. This is only one example out of many.

Negative thinking tends to block the ability for me to hear what the God of my understanding is bringing into my life. If I take time out for positive thinking and spiritual, inspirational reading, I experience a conscious attitude correction. I see glimpses of the world that I normally wouldn't have taken in; then I have the choice to integrate a part of those beliefs into my own.

We can be teachable by offering up simple prayers that don't ask for results or by not trying to understand what will happen before it occurs. I believe that prayer works in our lives by offering solutions indirectly through our relationships with others.

At one time I felt a lot of discouragement in working for a treatment center which was conflicting with my values. I remember making a prayer when I was on vacation and I saw a man fishing on a bridge. In my prayer, I said "I wish my life was as simple as his" and within a year my job ended with that organization. For another year I set up halfway houses for a Chaplain. After I completed my contract for one year, the Chaplain asked me if I wanted to take six months off to think about what direction I wanted to go. He had a house in the mountains that he would let me use that had been donated to him. I agreed and moved my family there for six months. It ended up being across the street from the bridge that I had seen the man fishing on a year and half earlier when I made that prayer. My life did get a lot simpler and more peaceful, but I never caught one fish from that bridge.

Of course those who believe can come up with countless stories. These stories don't justify belief for others, only for themselves. Faith is an un-tangible element that doesn't give us answers to questions; rather it gives us direction to find the answers. Can prayer change the outcomes on everyday situations? What I do know is that it can change my perception of the problem.

Believing that there is a God of your understanding who is watching out for you is comforting. This belief can make a person more open to other options because they believe that there are other possibilities.

Whatever ritual seems to be effective for us is important to recovery. In the morning, getting prepared for the day is a specific time people can look to prayer and meditation. Many people start the day by planning for it over a cup of coffee and reading a daily meditation book. Some may pray before going to sleep after reviewing their Tenth Step. As intelligent human beings, it is natural for our minds to shift to the negative, being pessimistic. As my day swells with other experiences, my interactions may become persuaded by negative outcomes, but I can always start my day again. I often carry a meditation book with me for that purpose. Prayer also can set the stage for that process to occur, by turning over your stress to the loving God of your understanding. It is important for me to share my true feelings during this time. I need to say with sincerity, "Thank you God for this day, for what you have given me, for what you have taken from me and for what is about to happen." The issue is not to just say the words, but to believe the words we are saying and have the emotional connection to what they mean.

Meditation is a way of silencing our inner thoughts which usually project us into past events or into future "what ifs." It is being in the moment and aware of that moment's existence. I used to be confused about what meditation was for, thinking that the God of my understanding would answer me in a lofty voice. Well, that never happened. But when I changed my expectations of meditation, I could clearly see the advantage in my staying in the moment as much as possible. I am not going to find my answers in the past and I am not going to find my answers in future events.

Once we have developed the ability to listen through these various exercises, we can take time to contemplate God's answer to our prayers (in silence, listening for God's answers to be revealed). God, in one definition, is Good Orderly Direction. If we are listening for God's answers, and not just ours which we hope to identify as God's, we should ask ourselves if what we think we are hearing is self-serving and just the same old perspective as what we have now. God's answers also can be revealed through our interactions with others.

There was a story I heard about a man who told his friend he had proof that God did not exist. When the friend asked how he knew, he reported that he had once been lost in a remote area in Alaska. It was getting dark and he was becoming frightened that he wouldn't find his way back. He asked God to help him find his way out, and he said God never showed up. The friend asked how he got out of the predicament and he responded, "Ah, some Eskimos showed up and directed me the way back." He had made no connection that God might have used the Eskimos to come to his aid.

Prayer strengthens our resilience in dealing with our own insecurities that we experience in relationships with loved ones. Saying prayers for loved ones offer us the understanding that there is a loving God in their lives as much as ours. Praying for others feeling sorrow and turmoil also is beneficial to this process. When we are saying prayers for ourselves, we have to watch out for those "foxhole prayers." That is, "God if you get me out of this mess I promise I will never doubt you again." I have caught myself being selfish in prayers and looking for solutions to problems without having to acquire the humility to work through them. We gain insight into our Higher Power's benefit in our life when we list the positive things God has put in our lives and offer thanks. I find showing appreciation and gratitude for my relationships with my Higher Power and in my personal life, bring me to a position of satisfaction and acceptance of the cards life has dealt me. So being in the moment is the benefit of seeing my Higher Power's work in action.

We all rely on other resources to give us our reality. You can ask for assistance from your sponsor, your mentors or others. Our changing perception of how God works in our lives is based on how we perceive He interweaves in our relationships with others.

I remember my father came home from work one day laughing. He worked as a heavy equipment operator doing construction work. He reported every morning he would ask a Native American co-worker what the weather was going to be like. He would look up at the sky and say "It's going to rain a little in the morning and sunshine in the afternoon," or something like that. This had been going on for five years. On the day that my father came home laughing, he said he had asked his friend what the weather was going to be like and the friend said he didn't know. My father asked him why, and he said "I didn't listen to the weather report this morning."

This living in the moment helps us decrease stress in our lives. When we take a vacation, we are taking a break from our past and our problems that affect our present interactions with others. After a vacation we feel relieved and nourished in our lives. One reason, simply, is that we are interacting with a new environment, seeing things that we haven't seen before. This activity places us in the here and now and gives us a heightened sense of exhilaration. No one can stay totally within the moment. We are free thinkers and are only limited to making improvements in this area; progress not perfection.

Working the Eleventh Step opened our minds to an increased understanding of a loving God as we may understand Him in our lives. This continued effort to be open to possibilities not only in the physical world, but in our spiritual beliefs gives us resources to achieve resolution in any area of our lives. This brings us to the Twelfth Step.

Step Twelve

Having had a spiritual awakening as the result of these steps, we tried to carry this message to other addicts/alcoholics and to practice these principles in all our affairs.

The first concept we need to delve into is *"Having had a spiritual awakening as a result of these steps..."* We wonder what that spiritual awakening was. It wasn't just one incident that brought us to our awareness of who we are today. This Step takes into account all of the work and all of the people who were part of our recovery. My first sponsor, Bill M., wrote one of the first books outside the AA organization about the Twelve Steps, called "Tools for Fools: For Alcoholics and other Human Beings"1971. In his book he explained the Twelve Steps as a relapse prevention model, calling it the domino theory. Once a person has worked the Steps and has come into recovery, they have to deny the principles of each Step before they would go out and drink. Henceforth the comment, 'what Step were you working when you took that first drink?'

I believe that working each Step has brought about change in the perception of ourselves, which was achieved only by working the Steps with others. This new found perception is derived from building unconditional relationships with others, breaking free from our controlling character defects. We can relapse if we reject not only the Twelve Step concepts that we have come to believe in, but also those loving, honest unconditional relationships we have built. These relationships have been sustained through our spiritual beliefs in a Power greater than ourselves; a loving God in however He may unveil Himself in our everyday lives.

This evolution of spiritual change began with the First Step, *'We admitted that we were powerless over mood altering substances or behaviors, that our lives had become unmanageable'*. Our addictions had left us in the shadows, isolated emotionally and spiritually bankrupt. Acknowledging that we were addicts/alcoholics shattered our prison of denial.

In the Second Step, *"Came to believe that a power greater than ourselves could restore us to sanity,"* we were ill equipped in trusting others. With our next breath of honesty in this Step, we were willing to ask for help. We were drowning men and women yet our voice was being heard. Humility began to grow in our relationships by asking for help from God and others in recovery.

In the Third Step, *"Made a decision to turn our will over to the care of God as we understood Him,"* we took action by embracing the unlimited resources that were available to us through our relationships in recovery. We were no longer afraid of taking the support from others and the loving care from the God of our understanding. The Third Step was the demonstration of building these new relationships.

In Step Four, *"Made a searching and fearless moral inventory of ourselves..."* we saw there are people who move forward with this Step who are the true heroes of recovery. People who show the strength to work this Step often will follow through with the rest. Our fear was overwhelming in looking at the damage we created in our lives. With loving support from others in recovery we moved ahead in this endeavor, with courage and drive we brought our past to the light of pen and paper. We listed the character defects that were both offender and victim based, and where we withdrew from others, which caused damage in our lives and in the lives of others. By completing this Step we have demonstrated the integrity and strength of brutal honesty which strengthened our spiritual drive.

In Step Five *"Admitted to God, to ourselves and another human being the exact nature of our wrongs"* we brought our past out by openly sharing it with our sponsor, mentor or counselor in recovery. We have also openly acknowledged our past to our Higher Power. In sharing all of our past, including our secrets with a person and our loving God, we disclosed our character defects and what impact they had on ourselves and others. We have taken the ultimate risk, to expose who we are entirely, to one person. This accomplishment showed us acceptance from another person and gave us the strength to accept ourselves. This allowed us to further build other unconditional relationships. As said before, this is like jumping into the deep end of the pool.

Through Step Six, *"Were entirely ready to have God remove these defects of character"* we became prepared to dismantle the character defects that sustained us in our addictions. We became aware of what we got out of our character defects, which was control, being controlled or withdrawing. What staying in those relationships cost us was being left alone. Our awareness brought us to the readiness of making personal change in our relationships with others in the present.

In Step Seven, *"Humbly asked God to remove our shortcomings"* we took the action of this Step to make the ultimate sacrifice: exchanging our victim, offender and isolating behaviors for new relationships with others based on unconditional relationships. We stepped beyond our perception of who we were to who we are becoming in recovery, based on our new found humility.

In Step Eight, *"Made a list of people we had harmed and became willing to make amends to them all,"* our new found humility brought awareness that we were responsible for the damage we caused in those relationships. This list identified who we affected through our victim, offender and isolating behaviors/character defects. We made the list with support of others around us. We broke through the last barriers of denial which were left in this preparation.

In Step Nine, *"Made direct amends to such people wherever possible, except when to do so would injure them or others"*, with assistance of a sponsor, counselor and other mentors in Twelve Step recovery, we pursued this effort guided by a loving God of our understanding. This action of amends and restitution allowed our relationships with others to heal. This process allowed us to reconcile our relationships with others, so that we could move on to unconditional relationships. This process included the amends we owed for being an offender to others, being a victim in other relationships, and being isolated from relationships. We faced and were accountable for our actions in our addictions and were ready to move on.

In Step Ten, *"Continued to take personal inventory and when we were wrong, promptly admitted it,"* our focus was in our present day in and day out relationships. We acknowledged responsibility when one of our victim/offender/isolating character defects flared up and we made amends. It helped us navigate through our daily activities, compelling us to use the program of honesty in our relationships with others.

In Step Eleven, *"Sought through prayer and meditation to improve our conscious contact with God as we understood Him, praying only for knowledge of His will for us and the power to carry that out,"* we proceeded with the teachable attitude that humility of the program had brought to us: to remain open to God's will in our lives. We allowed ourselves to be open to prayer and meditation in our lives, practicing it in our everyday activity.

This process that we have reviewed brought us to the Twelfth Step: *"Having had a spiritual awakening as a result of these steps…"* is often a gradual process unveiled to us as we work the Steps. The term "spiritual awakening" exemplifies clarity of purpose in ones actions. It shows a significant change has occurred in our life, giving us a second chance. For some, it may be an incident that triggers the awareness of this spiritual awakening.

I remember waiting for some type of burning bush to be validation that my life had changed. I was working at a man's clothing store and living in a halfway house at about ten months sober. One day I went out of the store to look at the work I had done in a window display and a young man approached me asking for spare change. I told him the street corners where he would have the best luck, and as he walked away I saw that he was me. Like me in the past, all he was looking for was enough money to get that next high. I looked in my reflection in the window and for the first time I could see that I had changed from the alcoholic/addict street kid into a spiritual being.

Our actions define who we are. We sometimes lack the insight to see the reflection of who we are becoming. Being aware of the changes that have occurred for the positive is important. Having obsessive compulsive characteristics in being an addict, we tend to focus on one thing at a time. In looking at our past actions we sometimes get stuck in an image of who we were and have difficulty in changing that perception to who we are becoming.

When I am at a Twelve Step meeting and introduce myself by saying my first name and I am an alcoholic and addict, I am telling everyone in the room the source of destruction that led me to recovery. I am acknowledging not only my pain of addiction and alcoholism, but my experience of strength and hope that have led me to who I am today.

Someone at a Twelve Step meeting told me once that this program is more elite than any other organization in the world because of what it cost us to get into the front door. As a result of being part of Twelve Step recovery, I also am part of a group of individuals that shares the same story. This part of the process makes me stronger. I discovered this not only by myself, but with others throughout recovery.

The second part of the Twelfth Step is *"We tried to carry this message to other alcoholics and addicts who are still suffering."* We have gratitude for the changes and spiritual awakening which has occurred in our lives. We relate on a deep sense of empathy the reality of pain and suffering that another alcoholic/addict experiences in their life. Our effort in sharing this experience with others is a continuation of our unconditional relationships with others. This common ground is the basis for our efforts to help another person suffering from addictions without judgment or condemnation. The effort of sharing on this level of interaction feeds our ability to regenerate further energy for our own recovery.

This energy, as to speak, replaces our initial motivation for change, which was fear and pain, to gratitude and hope. We see the pain of others suffering. Other addicts coming into recovery fuels further realization of gratitude for the changes that have occurred in our own lives. The power that empathy offers is a heightened awareness that the individual still suffering from their addictions is no different from us. We experience a sense of vulnerability that we are just a side step away from the devastations of addiction. This keeps us teachable in our relationships with others in our recovery and keeps our spiritual awakening alive. The effort of giving to others helps us build a more positive outlook in our own lives. We may get into ongoing problems, but taking time out to share with a newcomer gives us a new perspective on the simplicity of our issues.

We are responsible to provide support where it is asked. It is not our position to judge the person who is incapable of hearing our message. Even if a person has struck out at trying to stay sober countless times, it may now be their time for a shot at recovery.

The term 'principals before personality' also fits here. We must be spiritually fit to accept the responsibility of being a support to anyone who asks. Our ability to believe that anyone has a chance at recovery, no matter what their circumstances are, is necessary in order to provide assistance to another addict. Like us, they can see through our actions if we are talking down to them or judging them, and they may reject any help that is available.

Our effort to help someone else comes out naturally by sharing from our personal experiences in recovery. It is the strength that we have found through the diligence of working the program and the hope that we have experienced from the program working in our lives. This attribute offers our unique message to others in the framework, which allows the newcomer a non-threatening support. We are not there to give advice or tell them how to manage an already unmanageable situation. We are relating to their predicament and offering them the same resources that were offered to us. Our ability to respond with warmth and compassion comes from talking across to them rather than down to them. Our Higher Power is also working through us, and is there to guide us in the message we are offering. This is a vital energy resource that isn't just working through us, but is also filling us.

We present our message to the newcomer without reflection on how they may respond to it. Yes, we wish that they would be able to come out of their suffering and into the light of recovery. The outcome isn't on our time table. It is up to them and the loving God in their life on how it is received. This may be a seed that takes time to grow in the person's life, until they are prepared to walk in the doors of Twelve Step programs. Others may be incapable of hearing the message and die from their addiction(s). My purpose has been served if I have made an effort to share with others.

I demonstrate my gratitude when I provide service. We may be called upon by someone from a hotline service, a family member or a person walking into a Twelve Step meeting for the first time. Maybe we need to provide support to someone by introducing him or her to recovery. Often at a Twelve Step meeting the newcomer is greeted with an almost overwhelming invitation from those around them, and with a list of phone numbers they can call for help.

What usually happens at these meetings is people share the experience, strength and hope that they experienced in recovery. When going out on a Twelve Step call to talk to someone, we should bring another recovering person, such as a sponsor with us. Having another person in recovery gives us security if anything would go wrong. There are no guarantees that the addict we are there to help will take our message as support.

We listen to what pain motivated him or her in the direction of recovery and we offer support and sensitivity as they enter recovery. If we are asked by an addict's family member or friend to provide support and the addict is not aware of the request, be cautious. If someone isn't ready for the assistance, he may retaliate or become aggressive during this event, which is called an intervention. The best thing to do is to refer the friend or family member to a professional counselor who specializes in interventions.

Taking someone to a Twelve Step meeting also could be considered a 'Twelve Step call' if it is the person's first meeting.

I remember working a construction job and waiting outside my boss's house with a co-worker. He had heard I was in recovery and wanted to know about it. When I told him about the Twelve Step meetings I attended for support, he asked if he could come with me to one that evening. He became an active member of the program after that. I hadn't even realized I was doing a Twelve Step call, but that's what it turned out to be.

Being in recovery can be an active form of Twelve Step work because people see our actions and are encouraged by them.

I once worked with a police officer who was in recovery, whose job was to transport incarcerated individuals to court and other county jails. He reported that for years he shared his story with everyone he transported. True, they were a captive audience, but the message still got delivered.

Another form of Twelve Step work is doing service work, such as being a secretary of a Twelve Step meeting. The secretary starts the meeting and opens it up for discussion. Another duty might be simply putting on the coffee and helping to put the chairs in place.

In 1974, I remember in Minneapolis that there were a limited amount of Twelve Step meetings for people of my age who were alcoholic and addict, so I decided to start other Twelve Step meetings. I went to treatment centers across the city to invite their clients. My involvement helped me to build self-confidence and to build relationships with others in recovery. At other times, I have helped start other Twelve Step meetings, and each time people joined my journey, it brought me satisfaction.

Being on the list for hotline Twelve Step calls is a positive outlet and so is speaking at various treatment centers, hospitals and institutions. The service representative from your local Twelve Step meeting should have information about what you can do. I have conducted Twelve Step meetings in prisons and at recovery based institutions for years and enjoyed my involvement with peers who attended. I have always left these activities with a sense of zeal and gratitude for recovery.

In summary, each of us has special gifts and a unique way of presenting our message to others. Some may find their place in doing

Twelve Step service work by being part of committees for helping set up a recovery conference. Others may find the simplicity of being at the meetings in doing service work, being a secretary or chair person. Some may find their place by presenting at hospitals and institutions. Others may be strongest in giving people first hand encouragement through working a hotline or going out on a Twelve Step call. And of course, in walking our path we become an example for others through our actions.

The third part in the Twelfth Step is *"practicing these principles in all our affairs."* If we are truly going to become part of society, then we need to extend our efforts into every faction of our lives. If the process worked on our addiction issues, it probably can work on other areas of our lives.

I once had a conversation with a person in recovery, a successful business man and former lieutenant governor of the State I was in at the time. He said he used the concepts of Twelve Step recovery in his business ventures and they were extremely productive in building business associations with others. I am not going to say it will cure your hiccups, but it can work in any area where we are at an impasse.

Often people who have addictions have other health issues to consider.

I was a smoker and at six years recovery I addressed my addiction to smoking cigarettes. It took me several years, but using the Twelve Step program as my primary tool for recovery, I have not smoked since.

Personal health issues through our self-care of nutrition and exercise can also be an issue for people recovering from addictions.

At age fifty I had, over the years, gradually gained fifty-five pounds of extra weight. I addressed the issue related to my eating patterns as character defects which I needed to change. The Steps helped me develop awareness and take action on developing a healthy lifestyle using nutrition and exercise. I have dropped the weight and have remained stable at the same weight for the past six years. The consequences of me being overweight caused me to have high blood pressure, snoring and sleep apnea. All issues were eliminated by taking care of my weight and health. It wasn't simply gaining awareness. I had to quit old habits that I had developed over a long period of time.

You are not alone. There are a lot of resources available to those in building health awareness: nutrition stores, nutritionists, Naturopath doctors, and of course our family practitioner. A simple eating plan, which is good for most people, is the diabetic diet, which is low carbohydrates and low fat intake. Some people will walk for forty minutes a day, work out at a gym, swim, or run. It is essential to set aside time each day for some type of activity, as it is a self-nurturing act of kindness for us. Of course it is within our nature not to take action until we see it as a necessity, but by being aware of potential health issues we are more apt to take action.

Personally, I have found using the Twelve Step program very useful in the experience of raising teenagers.

I remember my children telling me that they had a higher IQ, believing that they were smarter than me. I acknowledged that, but said they wouldn't see the benefit of their higher IQs until they turned twenty-one years old.

When stress is impacting my ability to live in the here and now, I can use the program to decrease the impact it is having on me and my relationships with others. Yes I am acknowledging and accepting the problem at hand, but I am finding ways to live with it through utilizing the Twelve Step program. Other areas that can occur could be mental health issues and losses in our life that we were not prepared for.

Using the program to its full capacity is unlimited. If we take even ten percent of the energy we put into our addictions and divert it into our program, we would probably have a great program. Sometimes you hear a person say "Joe switched from being addicted to substances, to being addicted to Twelve Step meetings." The resources we put toward recovery aren't just transforming us into another addiction. Addiction is the burden of a cycle that is the basis of an insatiable need, it can never be filled. The addict then continues to make the same mistakes, expecting different results. The person in Twelve Step recovery is in a constant state of interaction, adjusting their values based on their changing needs. There are no scales to determine quality of life, but my ability to make choices that can change my course through a day, an hour, or even just the moment makes it worthwhile. As a result of working these Steps we have integrated them into our lives and relationships with others. Our lives make sense, and we have confidence in our new found freedom in recovery.

Twelve Step Sobriety/Recovery Facts

There is more to Twelve Step programs than the meetings and the Steps. Slogans and jargon are a contribution to the program which aids the person in their recovery. Each is a beneficial part of the program and we will discuss these other elements in detail.

Twelve Step jargon and slogans seem to be the secret handshake that ties recovering people together. Placing these slogans on your car or on T-shirts is a signal to others in recovery that you are one of them. It invites them to share their involvement in Twelve Step recovery. The words "I'm a friend of Bill W." or "One Day at a Time" on a T-shirt or coffee mug keeps the person focused on the necessary diligence needed in recovery. Slogans are an essential part of recovery. They are concepts that are easy to remember and important to be visible as a person is making changes.

I knew a man who was introduced to Twelve Step meetings because he bought a car and it had bumper stickers on the back that said things like "One Day at a Time", "Easy Does It", and "Keep It Simple". He was driving around a small town he had just relocated to and people started coming up to him saying they were in recovery and asking him how he was doing. He eventually had someone drive up to him and say, 'I'm on my way to a Twelve Step meeting, and do you want to join me?' He thought that everyone in that town must have known he was an alcoholic/addict, so he followed the person to his first Twelve Step meeting.

The addictive/alcoholic personality stems partially from what is known as obsessive compulsive disorder. This may be demonstrated by a "play hard, and work hard" personality. They are passionate people who tend to live in the moment. Not everyone who has an obsessive compulsive personality becomes an addict or alcoholic. However, most who do develop addictions will test positive for obsessive compulsive disorder on psychological tests such as MMPI, Minnesota Multi-Phasic Personality Inventory. People with these characteristics are passionate people, they become focused at the tasks at hand which may trigger a positive or negative affect on their attitude. That means it is important to be able to do mini-interventions throughout the day. Slogans can precipitate these and help the person to stay on track with recovery. "One Day at a Time" and "Just for Today" is simple concepts that tell an addict/alcoholic if their day starts out bad, they can start all over again in the next moment.

Sometimes the effort to stay abstinent from our addictions/alcoholism requires us to live five minutes at a time. If we get through the next ten minutes without acting out, those moments will grow into hours and those hours will grow into days, and those days will grow into weeks. The simplest answer tends to be the most important to the recovering person: Don't use/drink for that day. The terms "One Day at a Time", "Easy Does It", "Keep it Simple", and "Live and Let Live" are simple, little phrases that can help us because we are individuals who tend to try to force outcomes when the solution, in most cases, is just to let it happen.

There are certain prayers that tend to become icons in the recovery process. The Serenity Prayer: *"God grant me the serenity to accept the things I cannot change, the courage to change the things I can, and the wisdom to know the difference"* is used to open a lot of Twelve Step meetings. Often recovery members will have the Serenity Prayer on key chains or framed as wall decorations in their homes and offices. The Lord's Prayer often is used to close Twelve Step meetings.

Another popular slogan used in recovery is "God doesn't give us more than what we can handle." If we have gained a concept of a Higher Power, we can rely on guidance and assurance that the weight of our problems can be carried by that Higher Power. The poem "Footprints in the Sand" by Mary Stevenson, often is referred to in meetings and recovering addicts also have it on walls in their houses or offices. This simple story reassures people in conflict that there can be resolution to their problems. Sometimes addict's negative thinking during recovery boxes them in and they need something to remind them that there is a doorway out.

The Big Book of Alcoholics Anonymous calls alcoholism "cunning, baffling and powerful". Big Book of Alcoholics Anonymous, How It Works, page 58.

I had a client who was sober for seventeen years, but then he moved to a retirement area where booze was sold by the gallon in local grocery stores. He relapsed and within three months got a DUI, his wife kicked him out of the house and he broke his arm falling down intoxicated outside of his home. His story adds another word for addictions to the list: cunning, baffling, powerful and "patient." His addiction waited for him for seventeen years before raising its ugly head again.

Using the term of being an "alcoholic or addict" is part of the introduction people make at Twelve Step meetings. This acknowledgement gives people in the group awareness that you share the same reason for being there that others do, a desire to stop the addiction/alcoholism. People also often share their sobriety dates as part of their disclosure. In Houston, Texas for example, this seems to be the acceptable pattern for introductions, stating their name, addiction and sobriety date. In most places a person just says their name and addiction.

If you are a visitor to the Twelve Step meeting, it is appropriate to check if it is an open or closed meeting. Closed meetings are for people who share the same addiction, identifying themselves alcoholic or addict. Open meetings are for anyone who cares to participate**.** It would be inappropriate to go to a closed Twelve Step meeting if you are not an alcoholic or addict or if you are not willing to acknowledge that you are. Often people go to Twelve Step meetings because they have been ordered by a court to attend, so they should attend an open meeting. They will have slips that the meeting secretary will need to sign to prove they were there. Not everyone at Twelve Step meetings will accept that the person is there for good reasons if they have been ordered to attend meetings. I suggest that the person who objects thinks back to his or her own introduction to Twelve Step meetings. In most cases, people are introduced to Twelve Step meetings by some outside motivation such as family, job, finances or some other consequence brought on by the addiction. It's like in an old western movie where the saloon girl marries the farmer and moves out in the country with him. When she comes back into town and her old girl friends wave to her, she snubs them and says to her-self, "those harlots."

In the simple introduction of people to meetings, they may see the opportunity for change if they are ready within themselves. The old saying "You can lead a horse to water but you can't make him drink" is true, but he just might if he is thirsty enough.

If you are a chemically dependent person, by standards of recovery you also are an alcoholic. So if you begin to drink, your sobriety date is given up and you open the door back to addiction. If you are an addict and you go to an AA meeting, it is a sign of respect to acknowl-edge being an alcoholic, even if you never have demonstrated a loss of control in drinking. That's just the protocol. In the beginning of AA there were both addicts and alcoholics who participated in the meet-ings. It wasn't until the 1950's that Narcotics Anonymous (NA) was born, so the term alcoholic was shared by both addicts and alcoholics in participating in AA meetings, prior to NA. In NA it is frowned upon to call your continued abstinence from substances "sobriety", they recognize the term "recovery." Most AA meetings refer to continued abstinence of alcohol and other mood altering substances that you abused as "sobriety."

Every Twelve Step meeting is different, even though all Twelve Step meetings follow the Twelve Traditions. There are different per-sonalities and different structures, even different group consciences. I have never walked out of a Twelve Step meeting disappointed in the outcome. There is always something new and positive I walk away with. The different personalities are what make Twelve Step meetings unique and rewarding. When I go on vacation out of the area, I make it a point to find and attend a Twelve Step meeting of some type.

Having a home group that you attend weekly is important. A home group is a meeting we have committed to attend regularly and where we take part in the business and service portions. Usually there is time allotted for a business meeting at a Twelve Step meeting once a month. Keeping within the framework of the Twelve Traditions is the theme at these meetings and maybe used for voting in service representatives, other recovery activities and involvement in other service work. Service involvement may extend into the community by providing Twelve Step meetings at hospitals and institutions such as a county jail. This type of involvement is healthy for recovery to continue.

The Twelve Traditions are the concepts of protocol that Twelve Step meetings are based on and they help the Twelve Step meetings keep within the intended direction. This matter of being involved with the Traditions is an important part of your home group's inventory process. Further information on the Twelve Traditions is available in a lot of reading materials: "Twelve by Twelve" is literature from AA and NA has "It Works, How and Why." Twelve Traditions was borrowed from Alcoholics Anonymous for developing other types of Twelve Step meetings such as Al-Anon, NA, CODA, etc.

Our A.A experience has taught us that:

A.A. Twelve Traditions

1. Our common welfare should come first; personal recovery depends upon A.A. unity.

2. For our group purpose there is but one ultimate authority-a loving God as He may express Himself in our group conscience. Our leaders are but trusted servants; they do not govern.

3. The only requirement for A.A. membership is a desire to stop drinking.

4. Each group should be autonomous except in matters affecting other groups or A.A. as a whole.

5. Each group has but one primary purpose -- to carry its message to the alcoholic who still suffers.

6. An A.A. group ought never endorse, finance or lend the A.A. name to any related facility or outside enterprise, lest problems of money, property and prestige divert us from our primary purpose.

7. Every A.A. group ought to be fully self-supporting, declining outside contributions.

8. Alcoholics Anonymous should remain forever non-professional, but our service centers may employ special workers.

9. A.A., as such, ought never to be organized; but we may create service boards or committees directly responsible to those they serve.

10. Alcoholics Anonymous has no opinion on outside issues; hence the A.A. name ought never to be drawn into public controversy.

11. Our public relations policy is based on attraction rather than promotion; we need always maintain personal anonymity at the level of press, radio and films.

12. Anonymity is the spiritual foundation of all our Traditions, ever reminding us to place principles before personalities.

Twelve Steps And Twelve Traditions, pages, 9-13. AA Grapevine. © A.A. World Services, Inc. Reprinted with the permission of A.A. World Services, Inc.

When a person states "My name is John, and I am an addict/alcoholic", he doesn't say his last name because of anonymity and also due to the Tradition of 'principles before personalities'. Often you will hear the abbreviation of someone's last name in identifying an individual at a Twelve Step meeting, such as "Jerry S. is speaking at the Friday night speaker meeting."

Attending speaker meetings also is beneficial because people can learn from other's experiences of strength and hope. It may be presented in a humorous or inspirational way. Speakers' stories may link to an experience that they have had in their addiction and recovery. Usually speaker meetings are set at a specific time once a month in schedule, if a speaker is available. Speaker meetings are listed in a

Twelve Step meeting directory. Meeting directories usually are available through a community resource agency or counseling agency. Often there may be a potluck dinner that members share before the meeting. Potlucks, or combined meetings, may be advertised through fliers or hot lines. Alcoholics Anonymous, Narcotics Anonymous and other types of Twelve Step organizations are often found in local phone book listings, or listed over the internet.

Twelve Step conferences, consisting of speaker meetings and regular meetings usually are held over a weekend so they don't interfere with people's work schedules. Speakers at Twelve Step conferences usually are more polished than those from your local area. They often come from out of state or out of region and have presentations that carry a strong recovery message. The speaker chosen to end the conference usually is a spiritual one with a strong inspirational message. The message can be appreciated by people holding a wide range of beliefs, even those who are agnostic or atheist. There may be special meetings on specific topics. Most conferences are co-ed, but you can find some gender specific conferences.

People can do service work by helping to design these conferences well in advance. They are people from that community where the conferences are being sponsored and held. Often you find people with quality, long term recovery involved with this service work. This gives an opportunity for the newcomer to build strong, healthy relationships with people in recovery. They will meet regularly to get the conference organized. Also, when the conference is put on, members from that committee will hold responsibilities at the conference, in chairing/leading meetings and acting as hosts for the conference. Conferences generally have a dinner that is catered by a hotel or convention center. The dances that follow are well planned and something you can get dressed up for. There is normally a countdown of sobriety dates, from the longest period to the shortest. Everyone gets applause for their period of recovery, even the newcomer.

On specific holidays such as Thanksgiving, Christmas and New Year's Eve, there are marathon Twelve Step meetings in most cities around the country. These meetings last for 24 hours. Basically that means there are meetings starting every hour on the hour. They may primarily function as a conference with such features as a pot luck dinner, speaker meetings, and maybe even a dance.

Another support group is on-line Twelve Step meetings. Search engines can readily find an online Twelve Step meeting any time of the day. People can chat by having an ongoing written conversation.

Young People in Alcoholics Anonymous is another Twelve Step meeting. Age limits may be set for meeting officers including Secretary, Treasurer or Regional Representative. This guarantees that the representative holding responsibilities in the meetings are young people in recovery. These groups will sponsor their own conferences with the normal components, but there may be more outside activities geared toward a younger age group, such as dancing, skiing, concerts and other outside functions. Meeting with others in recovery who are about their same age, helps young people to adjust to the pressures they have to deal with in society, family and friends.

If English is your second language, attending a Twelve Step meeting in your primary language can be an asset to your recovery.

People are more likely to share their feelings in their native language. They may feel more comfortable and thereby express themselves better. Also, people from the same cultures and countries may have common values, which can make sharing easier and more valuable. Twelve Step reading materials are certainly available in most languages. You can order them from different Twelve Step organizations.

There is Twelve Step meetings set up for the gay community. The benefit of these meetings is for the recovering person to feel comfortable in processing issues surrounding their substance abuse. For instance a lot of the socialization for the gay community occurs at gay bars/clubs. This is acceptable for several members in their recovery group to go to a gay bar/club after a Twelve Step meeting, not to drink-but to socialize. For a heterosexual person to go to a bar/club after a Twelve Step meeting probably wouldn't be acceptable as part of their social networking.

Of course, anyone is welcome to any Twelve Step meeting without exclusion. The only requirement for membership is the desire to stop using/drinking.

Attending a gender specific meeting can be more comfortable for some people. It can be a safe place for women to talk about sensitive issues they would not discuss at a mixed Twelve Step meeting. I find it valuable for men to spend time with men in recovery and women with women. When we were growing up, we spent more time with others of the same gender and that probably helped our personal development. In recovery, there is a lot of new personal development happening and same-gender nurturing is healthy and helpful.

Another type of Twelve Step meeting is reading from literature in recovery and then speaking about the topic. This could be a "Big Book" meeting in Alcoholics Anonymous, or a "Basic Text" meeting in Narcotics Anonymous. One Co-dependency Anonymous meeting may have members read a segment out of "Co-dependent No More," by Melody Beattie and then discuss how it pertained to them. Another co-dependency meeting may use the "Codependency Anonymous" book or other literature.

A beginners group to assist people working on the Twelve Steps was initiated in the 1940's and it stalled in the mid 1950's. This beginners meeting took people through the Steps in four meetings.

This project was reported to have had astounding success in aiding people into recovery from alcoholism. It has recently had a comeback since a book called "Back to the Basics" by Wally P. was published. He researched this project from AA archives and by talking with some of the founding fathers in AA, and old-timers in recovery. As described in his book, the section meetings are:

1) Surrender, which consists of going through the first three Steps.
2) Sharing, which involves the Fourth through Seventh Steps.
3) Restitution, which is Step Eight and Step Nine
4) Guidance, which are Steps Ten through Step Twelve.

At these Beginners' Groups, usually called "Back to the Basics", people start the series together and do the Steps together. This helps the newcomers get to the core issues of recovery for themselves. I have seen people attend these meetings with a mentor or sponsor in order to share the work they are doing in the groups.

There is also Twelve Step meetings called beginners meetings that are not related to the Back to the Basics model. They simply offer newcomers a meeting to help orient them into recovery.

Professionals Twelve Step meetings are for those who have careers such as doctors, lawyers or others whose anonymity is the biggest priority for them. These meetings may not be listed in Twelve Step directories, but are passed on by word of mouth. I have found that for these types of people, being with other high functioning individuals who also struggle with addiction is helpful for their recovery. People known to drink alone or to be bingers tend to feel more comfortable in this type of support group.

There are a variety of Twelve Step meetings available but if you live in a rural area, you may have to contend to having just a few general Twelve Step meetings available to you. Certainly it is within your grasp to start a meeting if you would like to offer another possibility in the community. All you generally need to do is contact your Twelve Step General Service Representative (GSR) in the community and notify them of a meeting being started. The GSR will have available pamphlets, materials, and formats for starting a new meeting. You can also make sure it is listed with your local community directory for Twelve Step meetings. Of course it is advised if you are new to Twelve Step meetings, to have someone in long term recovery help you in getting it started.

Christian Twelve Step support groups have been around for a long time. Alcoholics Victorious has been in existence for many decades. These groups are best for supporting people of strong Christian fiber who are strong believers and are churchgoers.

Celebrate Recovery is a support group started by Saddleback Church. It has a strong momentum and can now be found in almost any city in the United States. The group follows the Twelve Step program, but with modifications to surrendering their lives over to Jesus Christ. I have found their family-oriented meetings to be a positive environment for recovery. The meetings usually are started with a potluck dinner followed by a short sermon/testimonial related to recovery and then singing. Afterward, they break off into small, gender-specific groups to help process areas of codependency and addiction. They also support a Step group which processes a Step per month, usually giving the person in recovery time to review and work the Step in detail within the group. It is recommended to have a sponsor to assist you working on the Steps from Celebrate Recovery. They have affiliated programs for children and teens available through local churches. Most of these meetings are held at churches across the country, but can be found at other community facilities. The benefits of being involved with a church or organization like Celebrate Recovery is that it encourages family values and helps people break out of anti-social behaviors. Listings of Celebrate Recovery meetings can be found on search engines or at the Saddleback Mountain Church web site in California.

Twelve Step meetings often are found in churches or other community resource sites. AA meetings can be held at an Alano Club: a nonprofit organization that has the sole purpose of providing space for Twelve Step meetings. People may choose to pay a small fee to be an honorary member, but the meetings are open to the public and are free of charge. There are usually rotating positions held by board members who also may be involved in putting on dances or other recovery oriented activities.

Alano Clubs can be open for members to socialize in, between meetings as well. This is usually set up as a non-profit organization by members of AA to rent a building and offer lower rent costs for Twelve Step meetings. The board members often serve for a year and then others are elected from the meetings at the location they attend. Often a recovering person can pay a small fee to be a member of the Alano Club, which provides a sense of belonging to the individual. That differs from a regular AA meeting hall, which usually is available only during meeting times.

There are Twelve Step Biker Clubs set up to help people who have had the cultural connection of being a biker, to remain sober and in recovery, and to carry the message to the still suffering addict/alcoholic. It is also open to anyone in recovery interested in becoming a member as part of their recreational/social interaction with motorcycles. There are also Biker oriented rallies for people in recovery which is a Twelve Step conference for recovery. At these conferences there is usually a run, or ride that people who have motorcycles can ride in. They start and end at designated locations. There are speakers and Twelve Step meetings at these conferences, which may include a dance, dinner and/or potluck.

In addition, there are conventions, round-ups and campouts sponsored by Twelve Step programs for their members. Having a recreational activity that brings a person a sense of joy increases the quality of one's recovery. I have been to some weekend roundups and found the experience joyous and invigorating. There usually is a speaker who shares his or her experience.

Twelve Step campout activities generally are set for a specific time each year when the weather is nice. They include a lot of family activities, plus there are campfire Twelve Step meetings that you can't beat. So break out the camping gear and get to know the other members of the meetings and their families. Campout activities, conferences and round-ups usually are posted at regular Twelve Step meetings. There are a variety of outside meetings and styles to choose from. Find meetings that you are comfortable in, but if you don't find one right away keep looking. It is common for a new member of the group who has introduced themselves to receive a phone list of people they can call for assistance. This gives the newcomer a doorway to asking for assistance from other members of the group outside of the Twelve Step meeting.

People in recovery get sobriety chips, recovery coins and key chains at different periods of recovery. Newcomers are given a 24 hour chip. People are given monthly sobriety/recovery chips or key chains, for each month of sobriety, and for a year of abstinence thereafter. Once chips are given out at meetings, there usually is applause for everyone who has been sober for that day. Some groups may have a cake at a meeting for a person at a certain period of sobriety.

Often birthday cards are given at the yearly marker of one's sobriety. These annual dates are called Sobriety Birthdays or Recovery Birthdays. I have seen having these tokens as rewards during recovery give people enough incentive to make it through difficult times. For me, getting a sobriety chip and a hug at a meeting from the person handing them out is a flattering and exciting part of recovery. It is a time individuals stand out from the group and receive "at-a-boys" for their accomplishments. I found that a sobriety/recovery chip in my pocket felt better than any paycheck ever did.

After the Twelve Step meeting, going out for coffee with your recovery peers is called the "meeting after the meeting." Building relationships with people outside of the meetings is just as important as what goes on in the meetings. We call this the fellowship of Twelve Step Programs. There is an intimacy that is built upon our association with others in recovery that is a powerful strength. Similar to Veterans who share a bond, this connection can be a lifelong friendship that is based on a commitment to break the chains of addiction. These relationships can be very helpful in keeping us on track.

Socialization is essential in building a network of support in recovery. Attending outside activities with the recovery group helps to build that fellowship. You may find people who have similar interests. If you like to dance, but don't feel comfortable about going to a bar that has music and dancing, you can go to a dance sponsored by a Twelve Step recovery group with people from your meetings. Going with others to concerts or outdoor activities can also strengthen your hold on recovery. Keeping a meeting list with names and numbers of people can be helpful.

However, this backfired on me once. I went on a camping trip to Canada with a friend from Narcotics Anonymous. On our way back to the States a border patrol agent noticed a Narcotics Anonymous meeting list on the dashboard of my friend's new van. They thought because we had the list, we were international drug dealers. They totally stripped the van, including paneling and insulation. When they didn't find anything, they just left, telling us "Now throw this stuff back in your van and leave." My friend was almost in tears over the damage that had been done. I helped him put his van back together again and at least we had a story to tell others.

In order to be serious about sobriety, we have to let go of our old friends who are not supportive and rebuild a new group of friends who can help us in our recovery. This can easily happen if we are open to building new relationships in recovery. The various activities that Twelve Step meetings offer give us that chance to meet the people who will support our new, healthier lifestyle.

Sponsors and old-timers in the program often suggest not starting a relationship with a new significant other for the first year of recovery. That's because most people in recovery are fragile and suffer from low self-esteem because of their addictions.

When two people have sex, at least one usually will walk away with some emotional feelings about it, which could cause difficulty in focusing on recovery. Quite frankly, in any social group even outside of Twelve Step programs you will probably run into a few people who have questionable motives. Recovery has to be the central focal point in this first year. Often, if two people from the same Twelve Step meeting start a relationship in early recovery and then it doesn't work out, one of them will avoid going back to the meeting. Support is lost and the person can relapse. *When I was in the Progress Valley Halfway House in Minneapolis, I started dating a woman and I fell in love with her. Yes, I can still feel the mesmerizing emotional feelings I had, but that was because I was in the beginning of recovery; so I was vulnerable and my feelings were more intense. When I was about to leave the halfway house, she dumped me. A friend I had been in-house with told me she had started dating one of the other guys there. I stayed sober. She eventually distanced herself from the recovery house men. Ten years later, when I was working as a counselor in another city, I was watching "The Phil Donahue Show" on television. He had as guests that day 'women involved with men in institutions' – and there she was. I was shocked and a little embarrassed, hoping she wouldn't mention my name, which she didn't.*

The point is there are people in any group in recovery who are using the environment to get into new relationships. We call them "Thirteenth Steppers." They reach out to newcomers and appear to have the intention of helping them in recovery, but their true intentions are to get them into bed. These people also can be found at Twelve Step meetings, churches and other organizations where people gather. That is one of the reasons they suggest in Twelve Step meetings to stay close with others of the same gender in recovery. Women will tell other women and men will tell other men about people who are potential dangers and should be avoided in recovery. From my experience in recovery, you generally find a lot more men in these roles than women. But as you saw in my own case, it still happens to both genders. People get attracted to one another and relationships begin.

I am not saying that everyone who gets into a relationship in early recovery has a bad experience.

I had a client who recently had a sobriety birthday of twenty-one years. I called to congratulate him. His wife answered and told me that he was not there, but she would have him call, which he did. She said they went to a Twelve Step speaker meeting where they both spoke at the night before. She reported at the meeting that they were both warned by me not to get into a relationship in the first year of recovery, but did anyway. Still, that is the exception. Most cases will not have the same result.

In most cases when two people get into a relationship in their first year of recovery it can be devastating. The lingering low self-esteem from the addict early in recovery can trigger a relapse if faced with the down fall of a relationship that didn't work. Also, in the first year of recovery getting into a new relationship can take the focus off their personal recovery. This diversion can be costly and can be a significant factor of a relapse.

When people get into a relationship, they need to deal with what that relationship has brought into their lives, good and bad. Yes, if two people in recovery in the first year get into a sexual relationship it might raise a few eyebrows. It doesn't make that relationship any less relevant than anyone else's. It is important to continue to work with your sponsor, build relationships in recovery and not to isolate from others. It is important to NOT moralize about this issue.

When I was working as a counselor at a Job Corps, I had two clients, a man and a woman, who were recovering addicts. I couldn't keep them in the same room or even in a group together because they would constantly verbally attack each other. They are happily married now and have four kids. In other words there is no right and wrong way to be in a relationship, we work with what we got.

This may seem like an abrupt ending to this chapter, because it is an unending process that we experience in Twelve Step programs. I have shared what my experience has been in recovery in Twelve Step programs and what I have learned from others in their process.

This new adventure that is before you will awaken your awareness of self, others and a God of your understanding. There are countless other areas of recovery that I hope you learn for yourself in Twelve Step programs.

The Benefits of Working
the Twelve Steps

The Twelve Step recovering community is a diverse group of individuals sharing the same goal: the desire to halt an addictive process in their lives. The amazing gifts we receive from following this program is a lifestyle replacement that is beyond our imagination.

Alcoholics Anonymous' Twelve Promises:
If we are painstaking about this phase of our development, we will be amazed before we are half way through . . .

1. We are going to know a new freedom and a new happiness.
2. We will not regret the past nor wish to shut the door on it.
3. We will comprehend the word serenity.
4. We will know peace.
5. No matter how far down the scale we have gone, we will see how our experience can benefit others.
6. That feeling of uselessness and self-pity will disappear.
7. We will lose interest in selfish things and gain interest in our fellows.
8. Self-seeking will slip away.
9. Our whole attitude and outlook upon life will change.
10. Fear of people and of economic insecurity will leave us.

11. We will intuitively know how to handle situations which used to baffle us.
12. We will suddenly realize that God is doing for us what we could not do for ourselves.

Are these extravagant promises? We think not. They are being full-filled among us - sometimes quickly, sometimes slowly. They will always materialize if we work for them.

Big Book of Alcoholics Anonymous, Into Action, pages 83, 84.

© A.A. World Services, Inc. Reprinted with the permission of A.A. World Services, Inc.

Remember this is a program of progress not perfection. We will see these benefits develop in our lives, some things take time.

Relationships with Family:

Living without our ingrained character defects offers new potential for having a family of choice rather than a family of origin. Choosing to recognize ourselves and others as changing human beings within our families, changes our perception of the family. By acknowledging the ability to have choices, we distinguish ourselves as having rights, which begins our journey of self-realization.

By having a sense of independence in our family, we then choose freely to bond with those family members. For independence to occur within our family does not necessarily mean adulthood. Yet, many times that process of separation from our enmeshment does not happen until then. When it does happen, we can create a bond with family members out of love rather than necessity. The joy within our hearts of being present in the moment with our families becomes a moment of intimacy that is like a precious jewel which we hope we will never lose.

We gain the ability to have acceptance of family members' turmoil. No longer is there a need to react in an attempt to absorb or repel the family member's pain. Instead we have the passion to be there to listen and watch life take its course. We begin to believe that there is a God, or loving force in the lives of family members which they can choose to use as they see fit. No longer are we bonded to family members by the emptiness of unmet needs, but instead through love and health.

Having children of my own, in recovery I accepted the responsibility to be there for them as a parent during their childhood. I am also there for them as a father later in their lives as adults, to listen, to love and to share the learning experience of life.

It would be arrogant for me to say that I have broken the chains of my family's dysfunction for me and my children. I assume responsibility for facing my character defects in my own life, but I cannot deny the reality of my own children having to face their own. It seems there has been a sickness impacting families in our society. It seems that family traditions, such as the family going to church on Sunday, or family re-unions and other such functions, have been dwindling from the new generation of families.

In recovery, a rebirth of the importance of family can occur. The family rituals which may have seemed empty can be reclaimed with value. No longer does the family ritual of the Christmas holiday and other activities meet with distress. The family dysfunction may have used these rituals as a container for the emptiness experienced in each family member's life. In recovery these rituals no longer carry the resentment and pain of unmet expectations. They can be filled with meaning and happiness.

Having healthy boundaries with family members is accepting not only our own limitations, but also accepting their limitations. In understanding our inability to resolve other family members' problems, we become more at ease in accepting their imperfections. We are able to appreciate the other qualities they possess. In recovery we come to a point where we can develop boundaries rather than walls in our relationships.

Relationships with Friends and Acquaintances:
The new challenges that recovery offers us closes some doors to potentially destructive relationships and opens new doors to potentially constructive and rewarding relationships. The benefits to the freedom to choose our relationships give us new possibilities in

understanding what friendship can be. No longer do we feel obligated to be there for others that are costly to us.

Our new friends we meet share similar interests in self-awareness and the need for intimacy. Their perspective is based on optimism rather than negativity. We may meet these friends at Twelve Step meetings, church, or other community resources. People who attend these meetings may share a similar purpose which they can enjoy with a sense of serenity and joy. It is interesting that, collectively, these new peers share a fellowship of recovery in healing their emotional and spiritual wounds.

Many times when I worked as a therapist with a group of people I thought only coincidence brought them together. But actually there were many casting similarities in their experiences and needs. As social beings we are attracted to others who share similar needs to our own, spiritually, emotionally and mentally. Sometimes we will experience a sense of intimacy and sharing within the circle of support which cannot be compared. Peer esteem could be identified as the joy of feeling part of a circle of friends. It is realizing we are no less than and no better than anyone else within that group. Each person in the group is regarded as having an inherent worth that is respected by all peers.

Because of the healing of our character defects, we are not trying to gain attention through inappropriate behavior. No longer do we avoid our own needs for the approval of others; and no longer do we need to neglect the needs of others to serve our own purpose.

Relationships based on Sexuality:

The reward of being free from our character defects within our sexual relationships opens the doorway to intimacy. The fear of potential abandonment and human suffering are no longer the basis for companionship. To feel the power of love as an interaction of physical and emotional expression becomes a positive expression of truth and harmony.

The journey of sexual reality involves intimacy, sensitivity and strength. Our needs and desires become as valuable a part of our relationship as our ability to serve and to appreciate the needs and desires of our partner's. Sexual intimacy can be identified as what we bring to the relationship, our resources, our passion and our presence. It is the capability of being who we are in a relationship, rather than what others expect us to be. It also means being capable of accepting our partner as who that person is without needing to change them. It is being present in the relationship where intimacy and appreciation can pass from one to another. In not using our sexual energy as a medication for temporary relief, we can express our sexual energy as part of developing a monogamous relationship, finding our soul mate whoever they may be.

Relationship to our Physical Self:

No longer do we have to create a physical barrier between ourselves and the rest of the world. Having physical esteem about ourselves, we don't have to compare our physical bodies to anyone else. We are now endowed with the ability to choose for ourselves which characteristics we wish to achieve for our own bodies.

We maintain our healthcare through staying involved with doctors, dentists and other health care professionals. Taking care of our bodies becomes a nurturing and loving process. No longer does exercise or eating plans have to be a form of self-deprivation and abuse. We gain awareness of our physical needs and take gentle steps toward self-care. We become teachable and seek out professionals and other resources that help us to build that awareness. We begin to construct healthy eating plans, with the understanding of progress, not perfection. We meet the challenges with assistance from others in the program which helps to develop consistency in our plan. We develop an exercise plan with assistance from professionals and other resources which is based on our physical capability and suitable to our interests. This plan is set up with a time commitment that works for the individual, which is to their satisfaction.

Self-care is demonstrated through following through with goals which have measurable outcomes that they are accomplishing. This measure of accountability is generating a good feeling about oneself which can be interpreted as physical esteem.

Relationship with Society:

We experience a freedom from our character defects in being part of society. No longer is there a need to be reactive to our external environment. Our expression of self can be creative and unique to whom we are.

We no longer need to be enslaved to the duty of our careers in establishing a sense of esteem in our lives. We no longer need to feel overwhelmed by a sense of emptiness and inadequacy in our careers. Our careers or work places become areas to practice J.O.B. (Joy of Being). No longer do we need to attempt to prove our inherent value to others or to ourselves.

Our financial indebtedness and need for more abundance materials becomes less important to who we are as human beings. We establish a sense of security in our inherent worth with flexibility in our expectations regarding financial goals. We abandon our need to set our financial and materials goals based on keeping up with our peers or the Jones'. We begin to live within our means rather than our expectations. We no longer need to present a false sense of abundance through our buying power. We take action in resolving any legal issues that are still out there. We are more conscientious about following laws that are part of the community. We no longer look at others with prejudice or malice as they are simply human beings like ourselves. We take a proactive role in our community by extending a hand where needed by others.

Relationships in Public:

Publicly we become less insecure in our sense of safety. We experience a sense of relaxation of our need to control those in our environment. There is a change in our behavior and attitude from driving in traffic, waiting for a table at a restaurant and waiting in a grocery store checkout line. We become capable of change in our presence with others. We recognize when we are about to react and halt our character defect which is about to emerge, or stop it before any further damage occurs.

Spiritual Beliefs

We strengthen our sense of spirituality through the experience of practicing the program of recovery through sincerity, open mindedness and courage. As said in the Eleventh Step, this offers us a sense of God's will for us and the power to carry that out. This gives the recovery person a tremendous sense of purpose that fills their heart.

Our belief in a loving God of our personal understanding is a vital part of spiritual esteem. One's faith creates an attitude of awareness in our sense of purpose in relationship to the world in which we live.

We become open and teachable to the lessons that life brings to our experience. The series of choices we make will lead us in the direction we need to go for our spiritual development. No longer do we need to fear the choices others make for their own spiritual growth, either.

We can open our eyes to religion and spiritual doctrine without judgment. Our past religious structure, or lack of, may have caused us disbelief in spirituality. Our spirituality now springs into new awareness and beauty. What may have been an imprint of a lifestyle similar to an unused children's color book can now be filled with amazing colors and highlights.

Definitions

Here is some of the slang used in Twelve Step programs that may be helpful to review:

Acceptance: Admitting responsibility for ones actions.

Agnostic: Not knowing if there is a God, but being open to it.

Big Book Thumper: A regular in AA who knows the Big Book inside and out.

Camel Chip: A chip (coin) signifying a person with long-term recovery.

Chair a Meeting/Chair Person: Take on responsibility to lead the meeting.

Chip: Sobriety/Recovery coin marking a certain amount of continuous abstinence.

Cleaning House: Getting your life in order.

Cross Talk: No cross talk (giving advice to someone who has just shared in a Twelve Step meeting) is suggested at most meetings.

Double Winner: Attending AA and Al-Anon meetings.

Dry Drunk: A non-drinking alcoholic who does not follow the program.

Easy Does It: Keeping your recovery simple and non-controlling.

E.G.O: Edging God Out.

Fox Hole Prayer: Praying for quick solutions, "If you do this for me God, I will…"

G.O.D.: Good Orderly Direction.

Going Out: Someone returning to active addictions/alcoholism.

Gratitude List: Making a list of things we feel grateful for in our lives.

GSR: General Service Representative for a Twelve Step meeting in your area.

H.A.L.T: Don't get too Hungry, Angry, Lonely or Tired.

Heavy Metal: A one year chip.

Higher Power: Power greater than yourself, sometimes refers to your concept of God.

Hitting Bottom: How low one goes before getting into recovery.

H.O.W. It Works: Honest, Open Mindedness and Willingness.

J.O.B.: Joy of Being.

Let Go Let God: Turning over control to your Higher Power.

Live and Let Live: Practicing acceptance of others.

Keep Coming Back: Stay involved in Twelve Step meetings.

King Baby: Someone who is self-centered, self-serving.

KISS: KEEP IT SIMPLE STUPID.

Meeting after the Meeting: Out for coffee with others after a meeting, building relationships.

Newcomer: Someone in their first year in recovery and attending meetings.

Normie: A term used by people in recovery about someone who isn't an addict/alcoholic.

Nudge From The Judge: Court ordered to go to Twelve Step meetings.

One Day at a Time: Keeps our commitment to sobriety in the present.

Old-timer: Someone who has been in recovery for a lengthy period of time in Sobriety/Recovery.

Pink Cloud: Feeling totally positive about your recovery, usually referencing the newcomer in their first year of recovery.

Playgrounds and Playmates: People with whom we used with, in our addictions.

Principles before Personalities: Using the program, not our ego.

Relapse: An addict/alcoholic who goes back to their addiction.

Retread: An addict/alcoholic who relapsed and returned to the program.

Running And Gunning: Addict/alcoholic who goes back to their addiction.

Secretary: Monitors the Twelve Step meeting, choosing a chair person or leading it themselves.

Service Representative: Someone voted into providing service for an elected term for a Twelve Step meeting, area or region.

Surrender: Turning over control of one's addiction and life over to the care of God of your understanding. (Third Step).

Thirteen Step: Getting in a sexual relationship with a newcomer.

Treasurer: Someone who collects donations and provides reports of resources to the group and makes out checks for rent and other meeting related costs.

Turning it Over: Turning over our control to our Higher Power.

Wet-Drunk: Alcoholic who is still drinking.